# NUTC_

# CRIMINAL LAW

AUSTRALIA
LBC Information Services
Sydney

CANADA and USA
Carswell
Toronto · Ontario

NEW ZEALAND
Brooker's
Auckland

SINGAPORE and MALAYSIA
Thomson Information (S.E. Asia)
Singapore

# NUTCASES

# CRIMINAL LAW

FIRST EDITION

by

PENNY CHILDS, LL.B., LL.M.
Principal Lecturer in Law and
Deputy Head of Law School
Middlesex University

London · Hong Kong · Dublin
Sweet & Maxwell
1996

Published in 1996 by
Sweet & Maxwell Limited
of 100 Avenue Road
London, NW3 3PF

Phototypeset by J&L Compositon Ltd, Filey, North Yorkshire
Printed in England by Clays Ltd, St Ives plc


No natural forests were destroyed to make this product:
only farmed timber was used and re-planted


ISBN 0 421 554606

**A CIP catalogue record for this book is available
from the British Library**

# CONTENTS

# TABLE OF CASES

# 1. *ACTUS REUS*

## Acts and Omissions

**KEY PRINCIPLE:** *The definition of some offences is restricted to liability for acts. In such cases, an omission is insufficient unless it can be construed as an act.*

### Fagan v. Metropolitan Police Commissioner 1969

The defendant drove his car onto a policeman's foot. This may have been accidental but then he deliberately refused to move. He claimed that the original act was not assault because he lacked *mens rea* and the rest of his conduct was an omission which could not amount to assault.

**HELD:** (D.C.) Defendant's appeal dismissed. Assault cannot be committed by omission. However, the assault was not complete on mounting the foot but continued until the car was removed. Therefore, failing to remove the car was not a mere omission but was part of a continuing act. [1969] 1 Q.B. 439

**COMMENTARY**
Assault is one offence that cannot be committed by omission. Others include burglary, robbery, gross indecency and constructive manslaughter. Fagan would have been acquitted if his conduct could only described as an omission. For other examples of the consequences and difficulties involved in categorising conduct, see *R.v. Miller* (1983) (see p. 3) and *Airedale NHS Trust v. Bland* (1993) (see p. 4).

---

**KEY PRINCIPLE:** *Where an* actus reus *can be committed by omission, a defendant who fails to act is only liable if under a duty to act.*

**KEY PRINCIPLE:** *A duty to act may arise through contract.*

### R. v. Instan 1893

The defendant lived with her aged aunt who died after the defendant failed to feed her or get medical help when she became unable to care for herself.

**HELD:** (C.C.C.R.) Conviction for manslaughter upheld. The defendant was under a duty because food was paid for by the aunt, who relied on the niece as her only source of maintenance. [1893] 1 Q.B. 450

## COMMENTARY

A common law duty could arise from the familial relationship, but it is doubtful whether such a duty arises where the parties are of full age and capacity. It could also arise because the aunt depended on the niece, who had voluntarily assumed a duty. Moreover, the court felt that the duty could arise from a contract, implied from the circumstances of the case.

## R. v. Pittwood 1902

A railway gate-keeper, whose duties involved shutting a gate when trains passed, forgot to shut the gate. A person crossing the track was killed by an oncoming train.

**HELD:** (Assize Ct.) The defendant was guilty of manslaughter due to the duty imposed by his contract of employment. It did not matter that the contract was between him and a third party (his employers). (1902) 19 T.L.R. 37

---

**KEY PRINCIPLE:** *A duty to act may arise from the close relationship between defendant and victim.*

## R. v. Gibbins & Proctor 1918

A father and his common law wife failed to feed his child who died as a result. They were convicted of murder.

**HELD:** (C.A.) Defendant's appeal dismissed. The father was guilty of murder, having breached the duty owed by parents to their children. (1918) 13 Cr.App.R. 134

## COMMENTARY

Duties can also be imposed by statute. The duty in this case, could today also arise as a statutory duty under the *Children and Young Persons Act 1933*.

---

**KEY PRINCIPLE:** *A common law duty to act may arise through the voluntary assumption of care.*

# R. v. Stone & Dobinson 1977

An aged woman lived with her brother (Stone) and his common law wife (Dobinson). She refused to eat and became seriously ill and bedridden. For a number of reasons, the defendants failed to summon medical help and the sister eventually died.

**HELD:** (C.A.) Appeal against conviction for manslaughter dismissed. The jury was entitled to decide that the defendants owed a duty to get help or to care for the deceased once she became helplessly infirm. The assumption of a duty could be inferred from the facts that both defendants were aware of her condition; she was a blood relation of Stone, living in his house; and Dobinson had undertaken the duty of trying to wash and feed her. [1977] Q.B. 354

## COMMENTARY
(1) Reference to Stone's relationship with the deceased suggests a common law duty based on special relationship but it is unlikely that a duty would have been owed if she had not been living in his home. There was no such relationship with Dobinson but she had apparently assumed a duty by trying to care for the deceased. Does this mean that Dobinson would have been under no duty if she had not acted at all? What about Stone?
(2) Other cases falling within this category are *Instan* and the common law wife's duty in *Gibbins & Proctor*.

---

**KEY PRINCIPLE:** *A common law duty to act may arise from creating a dangerous situation.*

# R. v. Miller 1983

The defendant accidentally set fire to a mattress by falling asleep with a lighted cigarette. When he awoke, he failed to take any steps to extinguish the fire or prevent further damage.

**HELD:** (H.L.) Appeal against conviction for arson dismissed. Arson can be committed by act or omission. Where defendants create a dangerous situation and it is within their power to counteract that danger, a responsibility arises to do so. Since the defendant could, without danger or difficulty, have minimised the risk he had created, his failure to do so amounted to arson. [1983] A.C. 161

**COMMENTARY**

(1) The case deals with the *Criminal Damage Act 1971* but is presumably of more general application (although it may be restricted to result crimes).

(2) The duty is simply to take reasonable steps (safely open to the defendant) and only arose because the defendant created the danger in the first place. Lord Diplock contrasted the case of a passive bystander who sees a fire and does nothing but is under no duty to act.

---

**KEY PRINCIPLE:** *A person may be discharged from their duty to act, incurring no liability for an omission thereafter.*

## Airedale NHS Trust v. Bland 1993

A patient had been in a persistent vegetative state for over three years. The doctors and family wanted to withdraw treatment and artificial feeding and the health authority successfully applied for a court order to do so. The Official Solicitor appealed on the basis that withdrawal breached the doctor's duty to the patient.

**HELD:** (H.L.) Appeal dismissed. In the light of the patient's condition and views of the medical personnel, the declaration was granted. Whilst a doctor was under a duty to act in the best interests of a patient, continuation of treatment was not always in those best interests. In this case, since there was no chance of recovery, withdrawing treatment would not breach the doctor's duty. [1993] 1 All E.R. 821

**COMMENTARY**

The case further illustrates the difficulties involved in classifying conduct as an act or omission. The court stated that it was always unlawful to take positive steps to end a patient's life. It was only where the case was one of omission that it might be lawful because no duty was breached. This means that liability turns on how the conduct is classified: is withdrawing treatment an act or an omission?

# States of Affairs

**KEY PRINCIPLE:** *Conduct must generally be voluntary. However, voluntariness may not be required where the* actus reus *consists of a state of affairs (or event) rather than conduct.*

## R. v. Larsonneur 1933

A Frenchwoman, required to leave the U.K., did so by going to Eire. She was deported from Eire and handed to the police in the U.K. She was convicted of "being an alien . . . found in the U.K." (without leave) and appealed on the basis that her return was caused by circumstances over which she had no control.

**HELD:** (C.A.) Appeal dismissed. The defendant was found in the U.K. after expiration of permission to be there and so had violated the conditions of her passport. (1933) 24 Cr. App. R. 74

### COMMENTARY
The case has been criticised since the defendant's presence was involuntary. However, the cause of the prohibited state of affairs was apparently irrelevant. A similar decision was reached in *Winzar* (1983), where the defendant was guilty of "being found drunk . . . on a highway", having been placed there by the police.

# Unlawfulness

**KEY PRINCIPLE:** *The word "unlawful" may be included as part of the actus reus of a crime.*

## R. v. Williams (Gladstone) 1984

The defendant punched the victim mistakenly believing that the victim was unlawfully assaulting another. He was convicted of assault occasioning actual bodily harm and appealed against the direction that his honest belief that he was acting lawfully was only relevant if based on reasonable grounds. Whether this was a misdirection depended (see Chapter 2) on whether the word "unlawful" was a matter of defence or part of the *actus reus* of the offence.

**HELD:** (C.A.) Appeal allowed for reasons explained in Chapter 2. The word "unlawful" was part of the *actus reus* of assault, with the prosecution bearing the burden of proving that the actions were unlawful. Therefore the defendant had made a mistake about an element appearing in the *actus reus* of the crime charged. (1984) 78 Cr. App. R 276

**COMMENTARY**
In *Albert v. Lavin* (1981) (see Chapter 2, p. 25), the Divisional Court held that "unlawfulness" was a defence issue and not part of the definition of assault. However, the Court of Appeal in *R.v. Kimber* (1983) (see Chapter 2, p. 23), disagreed. The court in *Williams* expressly disapproved *Albert v. Lavin* and confirmed *Kimber* (1983). This was further approved by the Privy Council in *Beckford v. R.* (1988) (see Chapter 14, p. 157).

# Causation—In Fact

**KEY PRINCIPLE:** *Causation in fact requires that the defendant's conduct be a* sine qua non *("but-for" cause) of a result.*

## R. v. White 1910
The defendant was charged with murder having put cyanide into his mother's drink with intention to kill her. Medical evidence established that her death was due to heart failure and not the poison.

**HELD:** (C.A.) The defendant was not guilty of murder, but he was, on the evidence, guilty of attempted murder. [1910] 2 K.B. 124

**COMMENTARY**
Whilst the decision (concerned with attempted murder) does not deal directly with the point, it is a good illustration of lack of factual causation. But-for his act, the defendant's mother would still have died and so he was not the *sine qua non* (cause) of her death.

# Causation—In Law

**KEY PRINCIPLE:** *The defendant's conduct does not have to be the sole (or main) cause of a result but it must more than minimally contribute to it.*

## R. v. Paget & Pemberton 1983
The defendant held a woman in front of him as he fired at armed police. The police returned fire, killing the woman. The defendant appealed against conviction on two grounds:

(1) the immediate cause of the death was the act of the police and not attributable to the defendant.

(2) the judge had misdirected the jury in saying that causation was matter of law rather than fact.

**HELD:** (C.A.) Appeal dismissed.

(1) The defendant had caused the death despite the actions of the police. A defendant "need not be the sole cause or even the main cause . . . it being enough that his act contributed significantly".

(2) Causation is a question for the jury to decide on the facts but must be decided in accordance with legal principles. (1983) 76 Cr. App. R. 279

---

**KEY PRINCIPLE:** *If an event intervenes between the defendant's conduct and the result, it may be a* novus actus interveniens *(a new operative cause), breaking the chain of causation.*

## R. v. Jordan 1956

The defendant stabbed the victim who died a few days later following treatment for the wound. The wound had almost healed and the immediate cause of death was the medical treatment, described as "palpably wrong". The defendant appealed against conviction for murder.

**HELD:** (C.A.) Conviction quashed. The direct and immediate cause of death was a separate and independent feature (the treatment) and not the stab wound. (1956) 40 Cr. App. R. 152

**COMMENTARY**
It was suggested that where death arose from normal treatment for an injury, the injury could be said to be a cause of death. However, this treatment was not normal and so broke the chain.

---

**KEY PRINCIPLE:** *An intervening event will not break the chain of causation if the defendant's conduct is still an operative and substantial cause of the result.*

## R. v. Smith 1959

The defendant stabbed the victim, causing internal injury. A medical officer, not realising the nature of the injury, gave "thoroughly bad" treatment. The victim died within two hours of being stabbed but might not have died if given different treatment. The defendant appealed against conviction for murder on the basis that the treatment broke the chain.

**HELD:** (C.M.A.C.) Appeal dismissed. Death resulted from the original wound which was still an operating and substantial cause of the death despite other operative causes. [1959] 2 Q.B. 35

### COMMENTARY

The court distinguished *Jordan* as "a very particular case, depending on its exact facts." *Jordan* was also said to be "very exceptional" (and *Smith* was preferred) in *Malcherek & Steel* (1981) (C.A.) where life support for two injured victims was disconnected by doctors. Since the treatment was "normal and conventional" and the original injuries were still operative, the court held that discontinuing treatment did not break the chain of causation. Also, note the view in *Airedale* that allowing a patient to die of a pre-existing condition does not, in law, amount to causing the death which is still treated as caused by the pre-existing condition. Overall, the distinction between *Smith* and *Jordan* seems to be that in *Jordan* the wound, having practically healed, ceased to operate. Any attempt to distinguish the cases on the degree of fault involved in the treatment should now be avoided according to *R. v. Cheshire* (1991) (see below).

---

**KEY PRINCIPLE:** *To operate as a* novus actus interveniens, *the intervening event must be independent of the defendant's actions, potent and unforeseeable.*

## R. v. Cheshire 1991

The defendant shot the victim in the abdomen and thigh. The victim developed breathing difficulties, necessitating a tracheotomy. Two months after the shooting, the wounds had practically healed but the victim died from complications caused by the tracheotomy. The defendant was convicted of murder and appealed against the direction that only grossly negligent or reckless treatment broke the chain of causation.

**HELD:** (C.A.) Appeal dismissed. It was a misdirection to focus on the degree of fault involved in the medical treatment but no miscarriage of justice had occurred. The complication from which the victim died was a direct consequence of the defendant's conduct which was still a significant cause of the death. This was not an extraordinary or unusual case where treatment was so independent of the defendant's conduct and so potent in causing death as to exonerate the defendant. [1991] 3 All E.R. 670

## COMMENTARY
Factually, the case is similar to *Jordan* since the original wound had ceased to operate. However, only treatment that is so extraordinary as to be independent of the defendant's conduct breaks the chain and *obiter* in *Cheshire* suggests that incompetence does not of itself render treatment "abnormal in the sense of extraordinary".

---

**KEY PRINCIPLE:** *An intervening event will not break the chain of causation if it is dependent on the defendant's conduct and not truly voluntary.*

## R. v. Paget & Pemberton 1983
(see p. 6)

**HELD:** (C.A.) In dismissing the defendant's appeal, the court stated that an intervention must be independent and voluntary ("free, deliberate and informed") to break the chain. A reasonable act of self-defence or self-preservation (such as the police returning fire) did not break the chain because it was an involuntary response, dependant on the defendant's actions. For the same reason, an act carried out in the execution of a legal duty (such as preventing a crime or effecting an arrest) would not operate as a novus actus. (1983) 76 Cr. App. R. 279

---

**KEY PRINCIPLE:** *An intervening event will not break the chain of causation if it is dependent on the defendant's conduct and reasonably foreseeable.*

# R. v. Williams & Davis 1992

A hitch-hiker jumped from a moving car and died from the injuries sustained. The victim had, according to the prosecution, jumped to escape violence from the defendants who intended to rob him.

**HELD:** (C.A.) Appeal against conviction for manslaughter allowed. An attempt to escape from a threat does not break the chain if it is within the range of responses which could be foreseen by the reasonable person. However, in this case, there was insufficient evidence about the nature of the threat to determine whether or not the hitch-hiker's response was reasonable. [1992] 2 All E.R. 183

## COMMENTARY

The case confirms the conditions applying to escape attempts: the defendant caused the victim immediate fear of being hurt; the fear was well-founded and caused the escape attempt in the course of which the injury was sustained; the response was a natural consequence of the defendant's action (*i.e.* reasonably foreseeable as likely to happen, bearing in mind the agony of the moment and any particular characteristics of the victim). Compare the decision with *R. v. Roberts* (1971) (see Chapter 4, p. 38) where there was sufficient evidence to suggest that the victim's response was reasonably foreseeable rather than "daft" or unexpected.

---

**KEY PRINCIPLE:** *An "abnormality" in the victim will not break the chain of causation, even if it is not reasonably foreseeable.*

# R. v. Blaue 1975

The defendant stabbed the victim who died after refusing a blood transfusion because she was a Jehovah's witness. The defendant appealed against conviction for manslaughter on the basis that the victim's refusal broke the chain.

**HELD:** (C.A.) Appeal dismissed. The operative cause of the victim's death was the stab wound and not her refusal of treatment. The chain was not broken by the refusal because "people must take their victims as they find them". [1975] 3 All E.R. 466

**COMMENTARY**
The rule, stated *obiter*, that victims be taken as found (which covers physical and other attributes) prevents a break in the chain even though it may be an unforeseeable "abnormality".

---

**KEY PRINCIPLE:** *If the defendant commits a number of different acts and the prosecution cannot prove which one caused the specified result, the defendant must be acquitted unless* mens rea *accompanied each of the acts that may have caused the result.*

## Attorney General's Reference (No. 4 of 1980) 1981

The defendant slapped the victim, causing her to fall downstairs and bang her head. He dragged her upstairs by a piece of rope tied around her neck, cut her throat, dismembered her body and disposed of the pieces. The prosecution could not prove which act caused her death and the judge directed an acquittal.

**HELD:** (C.A.) It was not necessary to prove which act caused death as long as the jury was satisfied that each possible cause was accompanied by the relevant *mens rea*. However, if the jury felt that any one of the relevant acts was not accompanied by *mens rea*, they must acquit even where satisfied that the remaining acts were so accompanied. [1981] 2 All E.R. 617

**COMMENTARY**
A conviction for manslaughter was possible because evidence suggested that all of the acts were accompanied by the *mens rea* of manslaughter. Contrast *Fisher* (1987) (C.A.) where the prosecution could not prove whether death was caused by hitting the victim or by dragging him downstairs. The defendant was acquitted because whilst the dragging was accompanied by *mens rea*, the blow may have been in self-defence.

# Contemporaneity

**KEY PRINCIPLE:** *The* actus reus *and* mens rea *of a crime must be contemporaneous (coincide in time). Where an* actus reus *initially occurs without* mens rea, *contemporaneity may* *be achieved if the* actus reus *is construed as a continuing act and* mens rea *occurs during its continuance.*

## Fagan v. Metropolitan Police Commissioner 1969

(see p. 1)

**HELD:** (D.C.) Appeal dismissed. The court confirmed that ". . . both . . . *actus reus* and *mens rea* must be present at the same time". However, lack of contemporaneity was avoided by construing the *actus reus* as continuing from its inception (when there was no *mens rea*) until the car was removed (when there was *mens rea*). [1969] 1 Q.B. 439

### COMMENTARY

For another illustration of this principle, see *Kaitamaki v. R.* (1985) (Chapter 5, p. 42). A similar problem arose in *Miller* (1983) where the act of starting the fire was not accompanied by *mens rea. Mens rea* was formed later when the defendant failed to act. The Court of Appeal adopted the approach in *Fagan*, treating the conduct as a continuing act so that *mens rea* was formed during its continuance. The House of Lords rejected this approach, deciding that the conduct was an omission and not a continuing act. They achieved the same result by holding that the failure to act (accompanied by *mens rea*) was the *actus reus.* This approach is only possible where the offence can be committed by omission and there is a duty to act.

---

**KEY PRINCIPLE:** *Where a series of acts culminate in the* actus reus, *and* mens rea *existed before but not at the time of the* actus reus, *contemporaneity is achieved if the series of acts are a continuous transaction connecting* actus reus *and* mens rea.

## Thabo Meli v. R. 1954

In pursuance of a pre-conceived plan to kill and evade detection, the defendants assaulted the victim. Believing him to be dead, they "staged" an accident by dropping the body over a cliff where the victim ultimately died from exposure.

**HELD:** (P.C.) Defendant's appeal against conviction for murder dismissed. The first act(s), done with *mens rea*, did not cause death and the act(s) which did cause death were not accompanied by *mens rea*. However, the acts were not separate. They were all part of the plan and therefore represented one series of acts during which *actus reus* and *mens rea* were present. [1954] 1 All E.R. 373

## R. v. Church 1966

The defendant was convicted of manslaughter, having assaulted the victim with intent. Apparently believing the victim to be dead, he threw her body in a river where she died from drowning.

**HELD:** (C.A.) Defendant's appeal dismissed. The jury was entitled to treat the series of acts as one course of conduct. Therefore, because the first act would establish (at least) manslaughter if the victim had died, the defendant was guilty even though he lacked *mens rea* at the time of doing the act that caused death. [1966] 1 Q.B. 59

**COMMENTARY**
(1) The court also felt that murder was possible if the series of acts were designed to cause death or grievous bodily harm.
(2) There was no pre-conceived plan as in *Thabo Meli* (1954) nor did the court explain why, in the absence of such, this could still be viewed as one transaction. Explanation comes in the next case.

## R. v. Le Brun 1992

In the course of an argument, the defendant hit his wife, causing her to become unconscious. In dragging her away thereafter, he caused her death by accidentally dropping her body. He was convicted of manslaughter.

**HELD:** (C.A.) Defendant's appeal dismissed. Where there is a time interval between the act done with *mens rea* (the original assault) and the act that causes death, there may still be a conviction if all the acts are part of the same sequence of events (the same transaction). This is easily established where the subsequent actions are designed to conceal the original act done with *mens rea*. [1992] 1 Q.B. 61

**COMMENTARY**
(1) The court distinguished *Thabo Meli* (1954) because there was no pre-conceived plan. Moreover, unlike *Thabo Meli* or

*Church*, the defendant did not believe he was disposing of a corpse.

(2) The continuous transaction principle dealt with lack of contemporaneity. Even if the second act was the sole cause of the death, liability arose because it was part of the same transaction as the act accompanied by *mens rea*. The court approved a distinction between subsequent acts by which the defendant was trying to assist the victim (such as trying to get the body to hospital) and acts not so designed (such as disposal or trying to conceal the original act). The latter established the continuous transaction whilst the former might not.

(3) The case also raises an issue of causation. If the first act is a contributory cause of the death and accompanied by *mens rea*, there is no difficulty with contemporaneity and the defendant is guilty because his subsequent acts do not operate as a *novus actus interveniens*. Acts designed to evade liability do not break the chain linking the original act to the death but acts designed to assist the victim might.

# 2. MENS REA

## Intention

**KEY PRINCIPLE:** *Aim, purpose or desire is a type of intention.*

### R. v. Steane 1947

The defendant was convicted of doing acts likely to assist the enemy with intent to do so, having made war-time broadcasts for the Germans. He appealed on the basis that he acted in order to save his family and not to assist the enemy.

**HELD:** (C.A.) Appeal allowed. The defendant's actions were consistent with the innocent intention claimed rather than the criminal intent charged because he had acted with the desire of saving his family from a concentration camp. [1947] K.B. 997

**COMMENTARY**

The court recognised that motive and intention are different concepts but the decision seems not only to equate the two but also to restrict the meaning of intention to desire.

**KEY PRINCIPLE:** *A result can be intended even though not desired (or wanted).*

## R. v. Moloney 1985
(see below)

**COMMENTARY**
In explaining the distinction between intention and motive or desire, Lord Bridge gave an example of a man boarding a plane he knew to be bound for Manchester. Although his aim (motive/desire) was to escape pursuit and he might not actually "want" to go to Manchester, he did, in law, intend to go to there because he knew that he was "morally certain" to arrive there. This recognises that intent has a wider meaning than that given in *Steane*.

---

**KEY PRINCIPLE:** *People are no longer presumed to intend the "natural and probable consequences" of their actions.*

## R. v. Moloney 1985
(see below)

**COMMENTARY**
The House confirmed that *Criminal Justice Act 1961*, s.8 abolishes this presumption. A jury is not bound to infer intention from this alone but must consider all of the evidence.

---

**KEY PRINCIPLE:** *Foresight of consequences is not equivalent to intention but may be evidence from which intention is inferred.*

## R v. Moloney 1985
A soldier shot and killed his stepfather in response to a drunken challenge. He claimed that he had not aimed the gun at the victim and had, at the time, no idea that firing it would cause injury. The judge directed that intention included both desire and foresight of probable consequences and the defendant was convicted of murder.

**HELD:** (H.L.) Appeal allowed, manslaughter substituted.

(1) The jury was not directed on the defence that the risk of injury had not crossed the defendant's mind at the time.

(2) The *mens rea* of murder (intention to kill or cause grievous bodily harm) should normally be left to the jury without explanation. However, in rare cases, judges should direct that intention might be inferred if the consequence was foreseen as a natural one by the defendant. Such knowledge or foresight was not equivalent to intention but was, at most, evidence of intention. [1985] A.C. 905

## COMMENTARY

The case establishes that intention differs from desire and also from foresight of consequences. The latter is simply evidence of intent and Lord Bridge gave five examples of the requisite degree of foresight which referred to levels of high probability. However, his model direction simply referred to "natural consequences". This caused controversy because of ambiguity in the meaning of "natural consequence": discussed in the next case.

---

**KEY PRINCIPLE:** *When considering evidence of intent, a jury must not only consider whether the consequence was foreseen as natural but must also consider its probability.*

## R. v. Hancock & Shankland 1986

The defendants pushed concrete from a bridge onto a road, killing a taxi driver. They claimed only to intend to block the road or frighten the taxi passenger and not to kill or cause grievous bodily harm. The jury was directed using the *Moloney* guidelines. An appeal against conviction for murder was allowed and manslaughter substituted by the Court of Appeal.

**HELD:** (H.L.) Prosecution appeal dismissed. Intention is determined by reference to all the evidence, of which foresight of consequences is just one factor. The *Moloney* guidelines were unsatisfactory because they omitted reference to probability. In addition to the guidelines, a jury should be directed that the greater the probability of a consequence, the more likely that it was foreseen and therefore also intended. [1986] A.C. 455

**COMMENTARY**
This refines the *Moloney* direction and receives further explanation in the next case.

---

**KEY PRINCIPLE:** *Intention can only be inferred if a defendant foresaw a consequence as a virtually certain result of conduct.*

## R. v. Nedrick 1986

The defendant set fire to a house, killing a child. He claimed that his intention was to frighten the child's mother and not to kill or cause grievous bodily harm. The direction was based on the law prior to *Moloney.*

**HELD:** (C.A.) Defendant's appeal allowed, manslaughter substituted for murder. Foresight of consequences is only evidence of intention if the defendant foresaw the consequence as being virtually certain. Foresight of any lesser degree of probability is insufficient evidence. [1986] 1 W.L.R. 1025

### R. v. Walker & Hayles 1990

The defendants were convicted of attempted murder having thrown the victim from a third floor balcony. They appealed against the direction that intent to kill could be inferred from knowledge of a high degree of probability of death.

**HELD:** (C.A.) Appeal dismissed. It was preferable to use the "virtual certainty" test from *Nedrick,* but the words "very high degree of probability" were not sufficiently different from "virtual certainty" to be a misdirection. (1990) 90 Cr. App. R. 226

# Recklessness

**KEY PRINCIPLE:** *"Maliciously" means "intentionally or recklessly" and recklessness, in this context, means realising a risk and running it.*

## R. v. Cunningham 1957

The defendant broke into a gas meter in order to steal the contents. Gas escaped, partially suffocating the victim. He was convicted of maliciously administering a noxious thing on a direction that "maliciously" meant "wickedly".

**HELD:** (C.A.) Defendant's appeal allowed. "Maliciously" did not mean "wickedly" but required proof that the defendant either intended injury or was reckless in the sense that he foresaw that injury might be caused but nevertheless went on to take that risk. [1957] 2 All E.R. 412

**COMMENTARY**
This purely subjective test (frequently referred to as "Cunningham" or "advertent" recklessness) meant that people who were incapable of appreciating risks were not reckless. Thus in *R. v. Stephenson* (1979), the defendant's conviction for reckless arson was quashed because he may not have appreciated or considered the risk of damage due to schizophrenia.

---

**KEY PRINCIPLE:** *Some crimes of recklessness are satisfied by proof that the defendant created an obvious and serious risk and gave no thought to that risk.*

#  R. v. Caldwell 1982

The defendant set fire to a hotel and was charged with, *inter alia,* arson contrary to *Criminal Damage Act 1971*, s.1(2). He claimed to have been so drunk that the risk of endangering lives had not crossed his mind. The question on appeal was whether self-induced intoxication was relevant to the charge.

**HELD:** (H.L.) Self-induced intoxication was not relevant for reasons explained in Chapter 14. Lord Diplock defined recklessness as including not only recognising a risk and going on to take it but also failing to give any thought to whether there is a risk when, if thought were given, it would be obvious that there was. [1982] A.C. 341

**COMMENTARY**
The decision confirms the "Cunningham" definition of recklessness but adds a second meaning (frequently referred to as "Caldwell" recklessness) which encompasses inadvertence.

# R v. Lawrence 1982

A motor cyclist was convicted of causing death by reckless driving. His appeal was allowed by the Court of Appeal.

**HELD:** (H.L.) Prosecution appeal dismissed due to a misdirection on recklessness. Applying *Caldwell*, a defendant was reckless if the driving created "an obvious and serious risk of causing physical injury. . . or . . . substantial damage to property; and . . . .the defendant did so without having given any thought to the possibility of . . . any such risk or, having recognised that there was some risk involved, had none the less gone on to take it." [1982] A.C. 510

**COMMENTARY**
This adds the word "serious" to the words "obvious risk". In *R v. Reid* (1992) the House of Lords decided that the requisite degree of risk did not differ in cases of advertent recklessness (where the reference is to "some" risk) and inadvertence (where the reference is to "such" risk, *i.e.* an obvious and serious risk). This was because the words "some" and "such" referred to the type of risk described (*i.e.* in this case, a risk of physical injury or substantial damage to property).

---

**KEY PRINCIPLE:** *Where recklessness is based on inadvertance, the risk must be one that would be obvious to the reasonable person.*

## Elliott v. C. (a Minor) 1983
A 14-year old set fire to white spirit, destroying a shed. She gave no thought to the risk and even if she had, it would not have been obvious to her because of her lack of experience, age, level of understanding and exhaustion. The magistrates ruled that "obvious risk" meant obvious to the particular defendant and the prosecution appealed.

**HELD:** (D.C.) Appeal allowed. The test was whether the risk would be obvious to the reasonably prudent person. It was therefore irrelevant that the defendant herself would not have appreciated the risk if she had thought about it. [1983] 2 All E.R. 1005

**COMMENTARY**
Goff L.J. regretted the decision but felt bound by *Caldwell*, *Lawrence* and *R. v. Miller* (1983) to hold that the test was "purely objective". Several of their Lordships (for example in *Caldwell, Lawrence* and *Reid*) object to the use of the terms subjective and objective, arguing that both types of

recklessness are states of mind (adverting and not adverting) and therefore subjective. That accepted, it is clear that the test for determining the obvious and serious risk is objective and not subjective. The test is also "purely" objective in that it is not (as in provocation) the reasonable person with the defendant's relevant characteristics: *R. v. Stephen Malcolm R.* (1984) (C.A.). This means that defendants such as *Stephenson* are now reckless. Indeed Lord Diplock overruled this case in *Caldwell*.

---

**KEY PRINCIPLE:** *A defendant who considers whether a risk exists and genuinely decides that there is no risk is not reckless.*

## Chief Constable of Avon & Somerset v. Shimmen 1987

An expert in Korean self-defence was charged with criminal damage having unintentionally broken a window. The court accepted that he was not reckless because, relying on his skill, he had decided that the window would not break.

**HELD:** (D.C.) Prosecution appeal allowed. Defendants are not reckless if they consider the risk and decide that there is none. However, this defendant had realised that there was some risk but had thought that he could avoid it. Thus he was reckless in the sense of realising a risk and going on to take it. (1987) 84 Cr. App. R. 7

### COMMENTARY

This so-called *Caldwell lacunae* was also recognised in *R. v. Reid* (1992) (H.L.). Defendants who consider a risk and decide that there is none do not fall within advertent recklessness because they have not decided to run the risk. Nor are they reckless in the sense of failing to think because they have adverted to the risk. Such defendants are, at most, only negligent.

---

**KEY PRINCIPLE:** *The Caldwell definition of inadvertent recklessness is not of general application in criminal law.*

## R. v. Satnam & Kewal 1983

(see Chapter 5, p. 46).

**HELD:** (C.A.) Recklessness as to lack of consent in rape is not satisfied by Caldwell-style recklessness. (1984) 78 Cr. App. R. 149

**COMMENTARY**
The same was decided in relation to indecent assault in *R. v. Kimber* (1983) (see Chapter 5, p. 52).

## R. v. Adomako 1994
(see Chapter 6, p. 65).

**HELD:** (H.L.) It was not appropriate to use the *Lawrence* direction on recklessness in the context of manslaughter. [1994] 3 All E.R. 79

**COMMENTARY**
This case deals with gross negligence manslaughter and so *Caldwell* may still have a part to play elsewhere in manslaughter.

## R. v. Savage & Parmenter 1992
(see Chapter 4, p. 40).

**HELD:** (H.L.) Caldwell-style recklessness does not apply to offences using the term "maliciously" such as *Offences Against the Person Act 1861*, s.20. [1992] 1 A.C. 699

**COMMENTARY**
The House gave no decision on assault and *Offences Against the Person Act 1861*, s.47 (although there is *obiter* supporting the use of *Cunningham* only). The Court of Appeal in both *Savage* (1991) and *Parmenter* (1991) suggested that Caldwell recklessness was not sufficient.

# Transferred Malice

**KEY PRINCIPLE:** *If the defendant has the* mens rea *of a crime and causes the* actus reus *of that crime against an unforeseen victim, the original* mens rea *is transferred to the actual* actus reus.

## R. v. Latimer 1886
The defendant intended to strike a man but accidentally struck the woman standing next to him. He was convicted under *Offences Against the Person Act 1861*, s.20.

**HELD:** (C.C.C.R.) Defendant's appeal dismissed. The defendant was guilty because "if a person has a malicious intent towards one person, and in carrying into effect that malicious intent he injures another . . . he is guilty of what the law considers malice against the person so injured." (1886) 17 Q.B.D. 359

**COMMENTARY**
The principle applies equally to offences against property.

---

**KEY PRINCIPLE:** *Malice can only be transferred if the* actus reus *(for which there is* mens rea*) is the same as the* actus reus *actually committed.*

### R. v. Pembilton 1874
The defendant aimed a stone at a group of people but it broke a window instead and he was found guilty of criminal damage.

**HELD:** (C.C.C.R.) Conviction quashed. Since there was no finding that the defendant was reckless about breaking the window, the intent to strike a person could not provide the *mens rea* for maliciously injuring property. (1874) L.R. 2 C.C.R. 119

# Mistake of Fact

**KEY PRINCIPLE:** *A genuine mistake about the existence of a definitional (*actus reus*) element of a crime negates* mens rea *whether or not that mistake is based on reasonable grounds.*

### Director of Public Prosecutions v. Morgan 1976
The defendants were convicted of rape although they claimed a mistaken belief that the woman was consenting. They appealed against the direction that they were only entitled to rely on their belief if it was both honestly and reasonably held.

**HELD:** (H.L.) Appeal dismissed. There was a misdirection but no miscarriage of justice. The *mens rea* of rape is intention to have intercourse without consent or recklessness, not caring whether there is lack of consent. An honest belief in consent negatives that *mens rea*. The mistake does not also have to be reasonable. [1976] A.C. 182

**COMMENTARY**

(1) The mistake is not a "defence" but simply denies the prosecution case. Whilst the mistake does not have to be reasonable, lack of reasonable grounds may be evidence that the belief was not genuinely held. This was the reason for applying the proviso on appeal.

(2) The court distinguished *Tolson* (1889) (see p. 24) and *Prince* (1875) (see below) as cases dealing with offences that do not require proof of *mens rea*. Cases of defences (where a mistake must generally be reasonable to excuse) were also distinguished. Thus, much turns on whether the mistake relates to a "definitional" (*actus reus*) element or a defence element. The same reasoning was used in *Kimber* (1983) (mistake about lack of consent in indecent assault) and in *Williams* (1984) (see Chapter 1, p. 5) where the word "unlawful" was held to be part of the *actus reus* of assault. Therefore even an unreasonable mistake about the lawfulness of the act negated mens rea. This was confirmed in *Beckford* (1988) (see Chapter 14, p. 157).

---

**KEY PRINCIPLE:** *A mistake about the existence of a definitional (*actus reus*) element of a crime is irrelevant (even where genuine and reasonable) if the element is one of strict liability and not afforded a defence of mistake.*

# R. v. Prince 1875

The defendant was convicted of abducting a girl under the age of sixteen. He appealed on the basis that he reasonably believed that she was aged eighteen.

**HELD:** (C.C.C.R.) Appeal dismissed. The statute did not specify *mens rea* in respect of the age. That element was therefore one of strict liability and since the girl was, in fact, under the age of sixteen the defendant was guilty. [1874–80] All E.R. Rep. 881

**COMMENTARY**

(1) The court distinguished other elements of the offence which required proof of *mens rea* (that the girl is in the possession of parents and that they do not consent to the taking). A mistake as to one of these elements would excuse the defendant.

(2) Not only did the statute not provide for *mens rea* in respect of "age" but it also provided no defence. Contrast *Tolson* (see below) and, for example, s.6 *Sexual Offences Act 1956* where the offence of under age sex is also one of strict liability but the statute specifically provides for a defence of reasonable mistaken belief in age.

---

**KEY PRINCIPLE:** *In some cases, a mistake about the existence of a definitional (*actus reus*) element of a crime, which need not be accompanied by* mens rea, *may excuse if based on reasonable grounds.*

## R. v. Tolson 1889

The defendant was convicted of bigamy. She remarried whilst her first husband was alive, genuinely and reasonably believing that he was dead.

**HELD:** (C.C.C.R.) Defendant's appeal allowed. The relevant statute did not require proof of *mens rea* in respect of "being married". However, it did not exclude (either expressly or implicitly) a defence of honest and reasonable belief that the first husband was dead. The defendant, who honestly and reasonably believed that she was no longer married, was not guilty of bigamy. (1889) 23 Q.B.D. 168

**COMMENTARY**
The court distinguished *Prince* (1875) where the policy behind the offence was such that there was no defence of reasonable mistake. It has been suggested that there are two ways of explaining *Tolson*. The first is that bigamy is, *prima facie*, a crime of strict liability but the defendant is allowed a defence of reasonable mistaken belief (mistakes in respect of defences having, generally, to be based on reasonable grounds). This is the view taken of *Tolson* in *Morgan*. The second explanation is that bigamy is a crime of negligence, so that a reasonable mistake disproves the fault element of the crime. Whichever is correct, the clear effect of the decision is that bigamy is a crime that can be committed negligently.

---

**KEY PRINCIPLE:** *Where a mistake relates to an issue of defence rather than to the existence of a definitional element,* *the requirements for successfully pleading mistake vary according to the type of defence in question.*

## Albert v. Lavin 1981

The defendant hit an off duty policeman in plain clothes, who was trying to restrain him to prevent a breach of the peace. The defendant mistakenly believed that he was being unlawfully attacked and so was entitled to defend himself. The question was whether he had assaulted the policeman which depended on whether he could rely on his belief that he was acting lawfully or whether he could only do so if it was based on reasonable grounds. This turned on whether the element of "unlawfulness" was a matter of defence or part of the definition of the offence.

**HELD:** (D.C.) "Unlawfulness" was a defence issue and not part of the actus reus of assault. Relying on *Morgan*, mistakes affecting *mens rea* are tested subjectively but mistakes relating to defences are tested objectively. Therefore the defendant was guilty of assault because his belief (as to self-defence) had to be both genuine and reasonable. [1981] 2 W.L.R. 1070

**COMMENTARY**
It is now clear that the analysis adopted (that "unlawful" was a defence element) is incorrect (see *Williams*, Chapter 1, p. 5 and *Beckford*, Chapter 14, p. 157). Therefore, where they affect the *mens rea* of a crime, mistakes about self-defence now fall within the key principle illustrated by *Morgan*. On the other hand, mistakes about duress and duress of circumstances have to be both honest and reasonable (see Chapter 14). Mistakes about provocation only have to be honest. In relation to defences provided by statute, the terms of the statute must be taken into account. So, for example, the "young man's defence" to the under age sex offence (referred to above) requires that mistaken belief that the girl is over age be based on reasonable grounds. In contrast, the defences of mistaken belief under section 5 of the *Criminal Damage Act 1971* do not have to be based on reasonable grounds (see Chapter 10).

# 3. STRICT LIABILITY

**KEY PRINCIPLE:** *A strict liability offence is one where* mens rea *or negligence does not have to be proven in respect of one or more elements in the* actus reus.

## R. v. Prince 1875
(see Chapter 2, p. 23).

**HELD:** (H.L.) The under age element in the offence of abduction is strict liability. Therefore any mistaken belief that the girl was over the age of sixteen is irrelevant.

**COMMENTARY**
Liability is rarely absolute, so generally fault is required in respect of some element(s) of the offence. In abduction, knowledge or recklessness is required in relation to the fact that the girl is in the possession of parents or guardian and that the taking is against their will: *Prince*.

---

**KEY PRINCIPLE:** *Where a statute does not refer to a state of mind, there is a presumption in favour of* mens rea.

## Sherras v. De Rutzen 1895
The defendant licensee served alcohol to a police constable, believing that he was off-duty.

**HELD:** (D.C.) Conviction quashed because the offence (contrary to s.16(2) *Licensing Act 1872*) required proof of *mens rea*. Moreover, generally "there is a presumption that *mens rea*, an evil intention, or knowledge of the wrongfulness of the act, is an essential ingredient in every offence . . ." *per* Wright J. [1895] 1 Q.B. 918

**COMMENTARY**
The presumption in favour of *mens rea* was also stated in *Sweet v. Parsley* (1970) (see p. 27) and *Gammon v. Attorney General of Hong Kong* (see p. 30). In the former, Lord Reid said ". . . whenever a section is silent as to *mens rea*, there is a presumption that . . . we must read in words appropriate to require *mens rea*." In the latter, the Privy Council listed a number of factors to be considered in determining

whether an offence was one of strict liability. The first was that "there is a presumption of law that mens rea is required".

---

**KEY PRINCIPLE:** *The presumption in favour of* mens rea *can be displaced by the words of the statute.*

## Sweet v. Parsley 1970

A landlady was charged with being concerned in the management of premises, used for the purpose of smoking cannabis. She occasionally visited the premises but was unaware of the cannabis smoking. She was convicted on the basis of strict liability.

**HELD:** (H.L.) Defendant's appeal allowed. The offence was not one of strict liability. Considering the words of the statute in question, the House decided that it must be the manager's purpose (intention) that the premises be used for the smoking of cannabis or, at the very minimum, it must be shown that she knew of the purpose to which the premises were put. [1970] A.C. 132

### COMMENTARY

The decision was confirmed by *Misuse of Drugs Act 1971*, s.8 which specifically requires proof of knowledge.

---

**KEY PRINCIPLE:** *The absence of* mens rea *words in the statutory provision in question, when* mens rea *words appear elsewhere in the statute, may mean that the provision is construed as strict liability.*

## Cundy v. Le Coq 1884

A licensee was charged with selling alcohol to an intoxicated person when neither he nor his servants realised that the purchaser was intoxicated. He was convicted on the basis of strict liability and appealed.

**HELD:** (D.C.) Appeal dismissed. Other sections of the *Licensing Act 1872* use the word "knowingly" whilst section 13, the section under consideration, did not. This was strong evidence that the offence was intended to be one of strict liability. [1884] 13 Q.B.D. 207

**COMMENTARY**
Contrast the decision in *Sherras* where the court accepted
that the presumption of *mens rea* may "be displaced . . . by
the words of the statute creating the offence . . ." but was not
prepared to infer strict liability simply because the section did
not use the word "knowingly" whilst other sections did.

## Pharmaceutical Society v. Storkwain 1986

The defendants were charged under *Medicines Act 1968*,
s.58(2)(a) with supplying medicine on forged prescriptions.
They believed that the prescriptions were valid and were originally acquitted but the Divisional Court held that the offence
was strict.

**HELD:** (H.L.) Defendant's appeal dismissed. Various sections
in the Act expressly provided for *mens rea* and so it could be
inferred that the omission to do so in section 58(2)(a) was
deliberate. Thus the offence was strict. [1986] 1 W.L.R. 903

**COMMENTARY**
Compare *Pharmaceutical Society v. Harwood* (1981) where a
prosecution under *Medicines Act 1968*, s.58(2)(a) for supplying medicine on an incorrect prescription failed because the
court decided that the section required proof of *mens rea.*

---

**KEY PRINCIPLE:** *Some statutory words are construed as
giving rise to strict liability.*

## Alphacell v. Woodward 1972

Pumps failed to work properly which caused polluted water to
overflow from the defendant's tanks. The company was convicted of "causing" pollution and appealed on the basis that the
offence required proof of *mens rea.*

**HELD:** (HL) Appeal dismissed. The word "cause" was not
accompanied by *mens rea* words and did not in itself imply *mens
rea.* It was a strict liability offence. [1972] A.C. 824

## Warner v. Metropolitan Police Commissioner 1969

The defendant was convicted of possessing amphetamine sul-
phate, found in a box in his possession which he claimed to
believe contained scent.

**HELD:** (H.L.) Defendant's appeal dismissed. "Possession" of drugs is a strict liability offence. It requires proof that the defendant knew he had control over something (which was in fact a drug) but not that he knew that it was a drug. Where the drug is in a container, possession of the container gives rise to an inference of possession of the contents. The defendant may displace this inference by proving that he was mistaken as to the nature (not merely quality) of the contents and; that as a servant or bailee, he had no right to open the container and had no reason to suspect that it contained drugs or; that as an owner, he received the package innocently and had no reasonable opportunity to ascertain the nature of the contents. [1969] 2 A.C. 256

**COMMENTARY**
(1) The court stressed that the meaning of "possession" might differ in other contexts. Whilst possessing a drug is strict liability, the case also provides a defence of lack of negligence in "container cases". The offence was re-enacted in the *Misuse of Drugs Act 1971* which specifically provides a no-negligence defence.
(2) Other statutory words have also been held to create strict liability. For example, "using" (as in using a vehicle in contravention of regulations: *James & Son v. Smee* (1955)). Other words import *mens rea*, such as "permitting" (or "allowing" or "suffering") and "causing" (as in causing another to commit the offence: *James & Son v. Smee* (1955)).

---

**KEY PRINCIPLE:** *If the words are not conclusive, the presumption of mens rea may be displaced by extrinsic factors such as the subject matter of the offence (including the stigma which it may attract).*

## Sweet v. Parsley 1970
(see p. 27).

**HELD:** (H.L.) In considering whether an offence is strict, Lord Reid added to *Sherras* that the subject-matter of the offence must be taken into account. According to Wright J in *Sherras*, the offence was one which was "not criminal in any real sense, but . . . which (is prohibited) . . . in the public interest". According to Lord Reid such "quasi-crimes" are less likely to require *mens rea* than "truly criminal" acts. When considering the latter, regard must also be given to factors such as the stigma that attaches to the offence, its gravity and whether public interest is served by strict liability. [1970] A.C. 132

## COMMENTARY

In *Lim Chin Aik* (1963) (see p. 31), Lord Evershed also referred to the relevance of the subject-matter in deciding on strict liability. He said that such liability was frequently inferred where the subject was the regulation of public welfare. However, deciding that the offence dealt with a "grave social evil" was not the only consideration (see below).

---

## Gammon Ltd v. Attorney-General of Hong Kong 1985

The defendants were convicted of offences under a Building Ordinance for deviating from plans and carrying out works in a way likely to risk injury or damage.

**HELD:** (P.C.) Defendant's appeal dismissed. The conditions to be considered in determining whether an offence is strict are:

(1) The presumption of *mens rea*.
(2) The presumption is strongest where the offence is "truly criminal" in nature.
(3) "the presumption . . . can be displaced only if this is clearly or by necessary implication the effect of the statute";
(4) "the only situation in which the presumption can be displaced is where the statute is concerned with an issue of social concern, and public safety is such an issue . . ."

Since the overall purpose of the Ordinance was the protection of public safety, the offences were ones of strict liability. [1985] 1 A.C. 1

## COMMENTARY

In *Sweet*, the application of these guidelines led to the requirement of *mens rea*, whilst in *Gammon* they did not. Likewise in *Storkwain*, Lord Goff was not swayed by the argument that *Medicines Act 1968*, s.58 was more than "quasi-criminal" and "would result in a stigma" attaching to the defendant. Other examples of issues considered to be grave social evils or matters of social concern are abduction:

*Prince*; pollution: *Alphacell*; and possession of drugs: *Warner*. In *Warner*, Lord Reid (dissenting) felt that the severity of the penalty, the stigma and truly criminal nature of possession were reasons for suggesting that it was not a strict liability offence. The remaining judges felt that the activity represented a grave social evil and that strict liability would prevent the object of the Act from being defeated.

**KEY PRINCIPLE:** *Generally, strict liability should not be imposed unless it will promote greater vigilance and assist in preventing the offence.*

## Lim Chin Aik v. R 1963

The defendant was convicted of contravening a statutory provision regarding entry to Singapore. An order prohibiting his entry was issued but there was no evidence that he was aware of this.

**HELD:** (P.C.) Defendant's appeal allowed. The offence required proof of *mens rea*. In addition to considering the social evil, regard must be given to whether strict liability would "assist in the enforcement of the regulations. . . . Where . . . strict liability would result in . . . conviction of a class of persons whose conduct could not in any way affect the observance of the law . . . even where the statute is dealing with a grave social evil, strict liability is not likely to be intended." [1963] A.C. 160

## Gammon Ltd v. Attorney-General of Hong Kong 1985

(see p. 30)

**HELD:** (P.C.) "The presumption of *mens rea* stands unless it can be shown that the creation of strict liability will be effective to promote the objects of the statute by encouraging greater vigilance to prevent the commission of the offence." Their Lordships concluded that imposing strict liability would help to do so in this case. [1985] 1 A.C. 1

### COMMENTARY
In *Sweet v. Parsley* (1970) (see p. 27), Lord Reid was influenced by the fact that even "the greatest vigilance cannot prevent tenants . . . from smoking cannabis . . . in their own

rooms" and Lord Diplock stated that "strict liability should not easily be inferred, particularly if there is nothing the defendant could do to improve, influence or control the situation". However, in *Storkwain*, Lord Goff rejected the argument that strict liability should not be imposed because it would not "tend towards greater efficiency on the part of pharmacists in detecting forged prescription."

# 4. NON FATAL OFFENCES AGAINST THE PERSON

## Common Assault and Battery

**KEY PRINCIPLE:** *The* actus reus *of assault involves an act causing apprehension of unlawful personal violence.*

### Fagan v. Metropolitan Police Commissioner 1969
(see Chapter 1, p. 1).

**HELD:** (D.C.) Deciding that assault cannot be committed by omission, the court defined assault as "an act which . . . causes another person to apprehend immediate and unlawful personal violence." [1969] 1 Q.B. 439

**COMMENTARY**
Apprehension of violence is satisfied by apprehension of battery (physical contact). Apprehension does not mean fear but simply anticipation of a battery. Despite doubts caused by *Albert v. Lavin* (see Chapter 2, p. 25), the actus reus includes that the force apprehended be unlawful, according to *Williams* (1984) (see Chapter 1, p. 5), confirmed in *Beckford* (see Chapter 14, p. 157).

**KEY PRINCIPLE:** *The victim must apprehend immediate force or violence. If the "threat" cannot be carried out immediately, there is no assault.*

## Smith v. Chief Superintendent of Woking 1983

The victim was terrified by the defendant staring at her from outside the window of her bed-sitting room. The defendant was convicted under section 4 of the *Vagrancy Act 1824* which, in this case, required proof of assault. He appealed on the basis that there was no apprehension of immediate violence because he was on the other side of the window.

**HELD:** (D.C.) Appeal dismissed. Although the defendant was on the other side of a window, the victim feared potential violence which was sufficiently immediate to establish assault. (1983) 76 Cr. App. R 234

### COMMENTARY

This provides a liberal interpretation of the term "immediacy". Also note *R v. Ireland* (1966) where the Court of Appeal held that fear induced by repeated, unwanted, silent telephone calls could not amount to assault.

---

**KEY PRINCIPLE:** *The* actus reus *of battery involves using unlawful force without the victim's consent.*

## Fagan v. Metropolitan Police Commissioner 1969

(see Chapter 1, p. 1).

**HELD:** (D.C.) Deciding that battery cannot be committed by omission, the court defined battery as the "use of unlawful force to another person without his consent." [1969] 1 Q.B. 439

### COMMENTARY

The term "force" is satisfied simply by proof of contact (or "touching", see *Faulkner v. Talbot* (1981)) and the force must be unlawful (see *Williams* (1984)).

---

**KEY PRINCIPLE:** *Consent to contact generally prevents liability.*

## Attorney-General's Reference (No. 6 of 1980)

Two young men agreed to settle an argument by fighting and one sustained a bleeding nose and bruises. The other was acquitted of assault on a direction that the agreement to fight (and the use of reasonable force) prevented liability.

**HELD:** (C.A.) Consent was no defence for reasons given below but "ordinarily if the victim consents, the assailant is not guilty." [1981] 2 All E.R. 1057

**COMMENTARY**
It was also confirmed in *R. v. Brown* (1994) (see p. 35) that consent may be a defence to assault.

---

**KEY PRINCIPLE:** *Fraud or mistake only vitiate apparent consent in limited circumstances.*

## R. v. Clarence 1888

The defendant was convicted of inflicting grievous bodily harm and assault occasioning actual bodily harm on his wife, having infected her with venereal disease during consensual intercourse. He appealed on the basis of consent and the prosecution argued that the wife would not have consented if she had known of her husband's condition.

**HELD:** (C.C.C.R.) Appeal allowed. The only cases where fraud vitiates consent is where it relates to the nature of the act or identity of the actor. The wife's consent was not obtained by fraud as to either of these factors and so there was no assault. (1888) 22 Q.B.D 23

**COMMENTARY**
More detailed discussion of fraud and mistake vitiating consent can be found in Chapter 5.

---

**KEY PRINCIPLE:** *Subject to public policy exceptions, consent is no defence where actual bodily harm is caused, likely or an intended consequence of the assault.*

## R v. Donovan 1934

The defendant caused bruising in the course of consensually caning a woman for sexual gratification. He appealed against conviction for indecent and common assault.

**HELD:** (C.C.A.) Appeal allowed. Nevertheless, the court indicated that, generally, consent was no defence where actual bodily harm was intended or a probable consequence of the activity. Public policy exceptions to the rule included "mutual manly contests" and "rough and undisciplined sport or play, where there is no anger and no intention to cause bodily harm." [1934] 2 K.B. 498

## COMMENTARY

For the meaning of actual bodily harm, see below. An example of one of the exceptions noted in *Donovan* is illustrated in *Jones* (1986) where "rough and undisciplined play", causing grievous bodily harm, gave rise to no liability because the defendants did not intend to cause harm and believed that the victim consented. In *Att.-Gen's Reference* (1981), the court held that consent was no defence where actual bodily harm was intended and/or caused because "it is not in the public interest that people should try to cause or should cause each other actual bodily harm for no good reason". It made no difference whether the fight occurred in public or private. The public interest exceptions included properly conducted games and sports, lawful chastisement, reasonable surgical interference and dangerous exhibitions.

## R. v. Brown 1994

The defendants caused actual bodily harm and wounding in the course of consensual sado-masochistic activities. They were convicted and appealed.

**HELD:** (H.L.) Appeals dismissed. Public policy and public interest did not require that the defence of consent be extended to inflicting bodily harm in the course of sado-masochistic practices. [1994] 1 A.C. 212

## COMMENTARY

The policy exceptions mentioned in *Donovan* and *Att.-Gen's Reference* were noted (and ritual circumcision and tattooing were added). The majority rejected the defence argument that the activities in *Brown* were of a sexual nature (in which case consent might have been a defence). In the court's view, sado-masochism was "violent", "cruel" and "degrading" behaviour and so there was no public interest in allowing consent as a defence. The court also approved *R. v. Boyea* (1992) (see Chapter 5, p. 49) where the infliction of (intended or likely) actual bodily harm in the course of sexual activity was held to be an offence irrespective of consent. However, note two later cases. In *R. v. Slingsby (Simon)* (1995), the defendant was acquitted of manslaughter, having caused the death of his sexual partner by engaging in an activity which caused serious injury and then death. Neither party intended or realised the risk of injury and the court held that consent to the activity prevented it from being an assault (and constructive manslaughter). Note that the parties were consenting to sex and not to actual bodily harm as such, which distinguishes the case from those cited above. In *R. v. Wilson* (1996), the Court of Appeal held that consent was a defence to inflicting actual bodily harm when the defendant burned his initials into his wife's buttocks (at her instigation). The activity lacked the extreme and aggressive element present in *Brown* and was akin to tattooing. Public policy and interest did not demand that such an activity, carried out consensually between spouses in private, should amount to an offence. On this vexed issue of the role of consent in criminal law, see the Law Commission's Consultation Paper (No. 139) published in 1995.

---

**KEY PRINCIPLE:** *The* mens rea *of assault and battery is satisfied by either intention or recklessness.*

## R. v. Venna 1976

The defendant was convicted of assault occasioning actual bodily harm, having fractured a bone in a policeman's hand whilst being arrested. He appealed against a direction that recklessness was sufficient *mens rea* for battery.

**HELD:** (C.A.) Appeal dismissed. The *mens rea* of battery "is satisfied by proof that the defendant intentionally or recklessly applied force to the person of another." [1976] Q.B. 421

### COMMENTARY
The same *mens rea* satisfies assault (intentionally or recklessly causing another person to apprehend violence). Moreover, according to *Williams* (see p. 5), the *mens rea* extends to the element of "unlawfulness" so that a belief that force is lawful denies the prosecution case. The *mens rea* similarly extends to "lack of consent". Recklessness in this context probably only bears its Cunningham and not Caldwell meaning: *R. v. Savage* (1991) (C.A.), *R. v. Parmenter* (1991) (C.A.).

# Offences Against the Person Act 1861, s.47

**KEY PRINCIPLE:** *Offences Against the Person Act 1861, s.47 requires proof of common assault or battery.*

## R. v. Venna 1976
(see p. 36)

**COMMENTARY**
Both this and *Williams* are cases of assault occasioning actual bodily harm under section 47 where liability turned on proving a common assault (or battery). The common assault/battery must cause the actual bodily harm in fact and law. For the rules on causation, see Chapter 1 and, for example, *R. v. Roberts* (1971) (see p. 38).

---

**KEY PRINCIPLE:** *"Actual bodily harm" is temporary or permanent bodily injury, not so "trivial as to be wholly insignificant".*

## R. v. Donovan 1934
(see p. 34).

**HELD:** (C.C.A.) "Bodily harm has its ordinary meaning and includes any hurt or injury calculated to interfere with the health or comfort of the prosecutor . . . it need not be permanent but must . . . be more that merely transient and trifling". [1934] 2 K.B. 498

**COMMENTARY**
According to *Boyea*, the degree of injury amounting to actual bodily harm changes according to social views on acceptable levels of injury (see Chapter 5, p. 49).

---

**KEY PRINCIPLE:** *Actual bodily harm includes psychiatric injury.*

## R. v. Chan-Fook 1994
The victim claimed psychological injury caused by the defendant. The defendant appealed against the direction that hysterical or nervous conditions could be actual bodily harm.

**HELD:** (C.A.) Appeal allowed. Actual bodily harm can include psychiatric injury (an identifiable clinical condition). It does not include mere "fear, distress or panic", and so there was a misdirection (and insufficient evidence to establish actual bodily harm). [1994] 2 All E.R. 552

**COMMENTARY**
The inclusion of psychiatric injury within the offence was confirmed in *R v. Ireland* (see p. 33). Also note that in *Chan*, the court criticised the *Miller* (1954) definition of actual bodily harm.

---

**KEY PRINCIPLE:** *The* mens rea *of section 47 is the same as for common assault and does not require proof of* mens rea *in relation to the actual bodily harm.*

# R. v. Roberts 1971

The defendant was convicted of section 47, after assaulting a woman in his car by trying to remove her coat. She jumped from the car, sustaining actual bodily harm. The defendant's appeal included the claim that it was necessary to prove that he foresaw that she might jump from the car.

**HELD:** (C.A.) Appeal dismissed. The prosecution must prove that the defendant caused the injury in fact and law. This was established since the woman's response was reasonably foreseeable as likely to happen as a result of the defendant's conduct. It was not necessary to show that he foresaw that this might happen. (1971) 56 Cr. App. R. 95

**COMMENTARY**
(1) The chain of causation is broken if the victim does something "so daft" that the reasonable person would not foresee it. (see Chapter 1).
(2) *Roberts* was approved in *Savage & Parmenter* (1992) (see p. 40) where the House of Lords confirmed that the prosecution only have to prove the *mens rea* of assault and not intention or recklessness *vis-à-vis* the actual bodily harm. Although the House of Lords did not deal with the issue, the Court of Appeal in both *Savage* and *Parmenter* indicated that recklessness in this context bears its *Cunningham* and not *Caldwell* meaning.

# Offences Against the Person Act 1861, s.20

**KEY PRINCIPLE:** *The actus reus of section 20 requires proof of either wounding or an infliction of grievous bodily harm. A wound requires proof that the whole continuity of the skin is broken.*

## C. v. Eisenhower 1984

The defendant shot the victim with an air pistol causing bruising and rupturing internal blood vessels in his eye. The defendant appealed against conviction for s.20 on the basis that there was no wound.

**HELD:** (D.C.) Appeal allowed. Breaking the skin of an internal cavity is sufficient where that skin is continuous with the outer skin of the body. A ruptured blood vessel in itself was insufficient evidence of a break in the continuity of the whole skin. [1984] 1 Q.B. 331

**COMMENTARY**
The epidermis and dermis must be broken for there to be a wound.

---

**KEY PRINCIPLE:** *Grievous bodily harm means "serious bodily harm"*

## D.P.P. v. Smith 1961

The defendant caused the death of a policeman who was hanging onto his car by driving the car into oncoming traffic.

**HELD**: (H.L.) In dealing with murder, the House commented that grievous bodily harm bears "its ordinary and natural meaning". The meaning of "bodily harm" was self-evident and grievous meant "really serious". [1961] A.C. 290

**COMMENTARY**
Grievous bodily harm can exist where there is serious psychiatric injury (*R. v. Burstow* (1996) (see p. 42)).

---

**KEY PRINCIPLE:** *The word "inflicting" in s.20 does not require proof that the grievous bodily harm was caused by an assault.*

## R. v. Wilson 1984

Two appeals raised the issue of whether a jury could return a guilty verdict under *Offences Against the Person Act 1861*, s.47 on a charge of inflicting grievous bodily harm. This turned on whether such a charge expressly or impliedly amounted to or included an allegation of section 47.

**HELD:** (H.L.) A verdict of section 47 could be returned on a charge of section 20. Allegations of "grievous bodily harm" include "actual bodily harm" and "inflicts" may include an allegation of "assault" although it does not necessarily do so because s.20 can occur "without an assault being committed". [1984] A.C. 242

### COMMENTARY

Lord Roskill appeared to agree that inflicting grievous bodily harm required proof of either assault or something resulting in "force being applied violently to the body". This latter requirement was doubted by the Crown Court in *Burstow* where the defendant had stalked the victim causing her severe depression. He was charged with inflicting grievous bodily harm under section 20 and submitted that he was not guilty because he had not assaulted or battered the victim. The submission was rejected and the court held that *Wilson* had simply decided that section 20 could occur without there being an assault. This had been confirmed in *Savage & Parmenter* (H.L.) where it was also held that a verdict of section 47 could be returned on a charge of section 20.

---

**KEY PRINCIPLE:** *The* mens rea *of section 20 requires proof that the defendant intended or foresaw the risk of some physical harm.*

## R. v. Savage & Parmenter 1992

Savage intended to throw the contents of a glass at the victim but let go of the glass, causing a wound. She was convicted under s.20 but because of a misdirection on the *mens rea* of s.20 of the offence, the Court of Appeal substituted a verdict of s.47. Parmenter was convicted of causing grievous bodily harm to his baby. Because of a misdirection on the *mens rea*, the Court of Appeal considered a verdict of s.47 but concluded that the *mens rea* had not been established and so quashed the conviction. Both cases raised the same issues on appeal.

**HELD:** (H.L.): Dismissing the appeal of *Savage* and allowing the appeal of *Parmenter* but substituting a conviction under section 47.

(1)   Both defendants could be found guilty under s.47, having been charged with s.20 (see above).

(2)   s.47 could be established even though the defendant did not intend actual bodily harm nor was reckless as to causing it. Therefore both defendants could be convicted under s.47 (and the Court of Appeal had reached the wrong conclusion in the case of Parmenter).

(3)   It was not necessary, under s.20, to prove that the defendant intended or foresaw a wound or serious physical injury. Intention or recklessness as to some physical harm, albeit minor, was sufficient. [1992] 1 A.C. 699

## COMMENTARY

The House also confirmed that recklessness in the context of s.20 (which refers to the term "maliciously") means foresight of the risk of harm and is not satisfied by Caldwell-style recklessness.

# Offences Against the Person Act 1861, s.18

**KEY PRINCIPLE:** *s.18, like s.20, requires proof of a wound or grievous bodily harm but, unlike s.20, refers to causing rather than inflicting grievous bodily harm. The word "cause" is wider than the word "inflict".*

## R. v. Mandair 1994

The defendant caused serious injury to his wife. He was charged under s.18 with causing grievous bodily harm with intent and found guilty of causing grievous bodily harm contrary to s.20 on a direction that this was an alternative, lesser verdict open to the jury.

**HELD:** (H.L.) "Causing grievous bodily harm" (s.18) could occur by inflicting the harm or by causing it in some other way. Since the word "cause" was wide enough to cover "infliction" (s.20), a verdict under s.20 was possible on a charge under s.18. Although the verdict of "causing grievous bodily harm contrary to s.20" was inappropriately worded since the offence under s.20 is one of "inflicting grievous bodily harm", there had been no miscarriage of justice since its totality made it clear that the verdict was for causing grievous bodily harm by its infliction. [1994] 2 W.L.R. 700

**COMMENTARY**
(1) Whilst this case suggests a difference between "causing" and "inflicting" grievous bodily harm, it may be that, following *Burstow* there is now little difference (if any) between them.
(2) s.18 requires proof of an ulterior intention to cause grievous bodily harm or to resist or prevent arrest. Unlike section 20, the section 18 offence is not satisfied by any lesser *mens rea* although foresight of virtual certainty is evidence of this ulterior intent: *R. v. Bryson* (1985).

---

# 5. SEXUAL OFFENCES

## Rape: The *Actus Reus*

KEY PRINCIPLE: *Sexual intercourse is established by proof of penetration but continues until withdrawal.*

### Kaitamaki v. R. 1985
Penetration occurred with consent (or belief in consent) but the defendant continued to have intercourse once aware that the woman was not consenting. He appealed against conviction, claiming that all elements of rape must be present on penetration.

**HELD:** (P.C.) Appeal dismissed. The New Zealand equivalent of *Sexual Offences Act 1956*, s.44 provides that sexual intercourse is "complete" (not "completed") on penetration. Since intercourse is only "completed" on withdrawal, rape can be established at any point prior to withdrawal. [1985] A.C. 147

**COMMENTARY**
The case confirms that rape can be committed by failure to withdraw.

---

KEY PRINCIPLE: *Sexual intercourse with any woman without consent is unlawful so that a husband who has non-*

*consensual sexual intercourse with his wife may be charged with rape.*

## R. v. R. 1992

The defendant attempted to have sexual intercourse with his estranged wife without her consent.

**HELD:** (H.L.) The marital rape exemption was no longer justified because of the changed status of women in marriage. The expression "unlawful sexual intercourse" did not mean intercourse "outside the bonds of marriage" and the word "unlawful" was "mere surplusage". [1992] 1 A.C. 599

### COMMENTARY
The case rejects the proposition of irrevocable marital consent (Hale C.J.). R. is now confirmed by section 142 of the *Criminal Justice and Public Order Act 1994* which removes "unlawful" from the definition of sexual intercourse in rape (and procuring under sections 2 & 3 of the *Sexual Offences Act 1956*).

---

**KEY PRINCIPLE:** *It is sufficient to prove that, in fact, the woman did not consent to intercourse. Consent may be absent even where there is no force, fear of force or fraud.*

## R. v. Olugboja 1982

The appellant had sexual intercourse with a 16-year old who was too frightened to resist although she had not been threatened with force or violence.

**HELD:** (C.A.) Appeal dismissed. Constraint on a woman's will (without force, fear of force or fraud) could negative consent. Consent is a question of fact for a jury who should consider its ordinary meaning and, if necessary, be directed on the distinction between consent and submission. [1982] Q.B. 320

### COMMENTARY
The case approves the distinction from *R. v. Day* (1841) between consent (which disproves rape) and submission (which does not) and confirms that the question is simply one of "lack of consent". This was applied in *R. v. Larter & Castleton* (1995) (case of rape of a 14-year old who did not resist because she was asleep).

---

**KEY PRINCIPLE:** *Apparent consent to the act of sexual intercourse is no defence if obtained by fraud as to the nature of the act.*

# R. v. Flattery 1877

A 19-year old submitted to sexual intercourse because the defendant defrauded her into believing that the act was a surgical operation.

**HELD:** (C.C.C.R.) The woman consented to the performance of a surgical operation without understanding that the act was sexual intercourse. Therefore she had not consented to sexual intercourse and so the defendant was guilty of rape. [1877] 2 Q.B.D. 410

### COMMENTARY
In *R. v. Williams* (1923) a choirmaster was convicted of rape having obtained submission by pretending that the act was an operation. The Court of Appeal confirmed that *Flattery* still applied despite the introduction of the offence of procuring (consensual and non-consensual) sexual intercourse by false pretence or representation (now *Sexual Offences Act 1956*, s.3).

---

**KEY PRINCIPLE:** *Apparent consent to sexual intercourse may be vitiated by fraud (or mistake) as to the identity of the actor performing the intercourse.*

# R. v. Elbekkay 1995

A woman consented to penetration in the belief that the defendant was her cohabitee. The defendant appealed against conviction on the basis that whilst rape included intercourse obtained by impersonation of a husband (*Sexual Offences Act 1956*, s.1(2)), the same did not apply to other cases of impersonation.

**HELD:** (C.A.) Appeal dismissed. The question was simply whether the woman consented (*Olugboja*) and she had not consented to intercourse with the defendant in this case. [1995] Crim. L.R. 163

### COMMENTARY
The case dispels doubts about consent obtained by partner impersonation and is supported, *obiter*, in *R. v. Linekar* (1995).

However, consider whether section 142(3) of the *Criminal Justice and Public Order Act 1994* precludes a similar finding in the future.

---

**KEY PRINCIPLE:** *Fraud (or mistake) as to matters other than the nature of the act or identity of the actor do not vitiate consent to sexual intercourse.*

## R. v. Linekar 1995

The defendant was convicted of rape on the basis that the woman's consent was vitiated by him defrauding her into believing that he would pay for the intercourse.

**HELD:** (C.A.) Defendant's appeal allowed. Since the woman had consented to what she knew was sexual intercourse with the particular man in question, the false pretence about payment did not vitiate her consent. [1995] 2 W.L.R. 237

### COMMENTARY
The court suggested, *obiter*, that on the facts of the case, a charge might have succeeded under *Sexual Offences Act 1956*, s.3.

# Rape: The *Mens Rea*

**KEY PRINCIPLE:** *The* mens rea *of rape (knowledge or recklessness as to lack of consent) is disproved if a defendant honestly (albeit unreasonably) believes that the woman is consenting.*

## D.P.P. v. Morgan 1976
(see Chapter 2, p. 22)

**HELD:** (H.L.) Honest mistaken belief in consent is inconsistent with the *mens rea* of rape (described by Lord Hailsham as "intention to have sexual intercourse without consent or recklessly" doing so). The reasonableness of the belief is only relevant as a matter of evidence. [1976] A.C.182

### COMMENTARY
Mistaken belief in consent does not have to be based on reasonable grounds which is consistent with the fact that

rape requires proof of *mens rea* rather than being satisfied by negligence.

---

**KEY PRINCIPLE:** *Recklessness in the context of rape does not bear the "Caldwell/Lawrence" objective meaning.*

## R. v. Satnam & Kewal 1983

Two men had non-consensual sexual intercourse with a 13-year old. They were convicted of rape on the basis of recklessness as to lack of consent and appealed on two grounds:

(1) The judge erred in not directing that recklessness was absent if there was genuine belief in consent.

(2) The judge misdirected on the meaning of recklessness by stating that it was sufficient to show that it be obvious to the ordinary observer that there was no consent.

**HELD:** (C.A.) Appeal allowed.

(1) There should have been a direction as to the relevance of mistaken belief in consent.

(2) The direction on recklessness should be based on *Morgan* and s.1 of the *Sexual Offences Act 1976* not on *Caldwell* and *Lawrence*. Recklessness required proof that the defendant could not care less about consent and pressed on regardless, not believing that the woman consented. (1984) 78 Cr. App. R 149

# Indecent Assault—The *Actus Reus*

**KEY PRINCIPLE:** *Common assault or battery is an essential element of indecent assault.*

## Fairclough v. Whipp 1951

The defendant invited a nine-year old to touch his exposed penis.

**HELD:** (D.C.) The defendant was not guilty of indecent assault by simply inviting the child to touch him because, since he had neither touched nor threatened her, the element of assault or battery was missing. [1951] 2 All E.R. 834

**COMMENTARY**

Whilst an invitation to touch is not indecent assault, the conduct (if "grossly indecent") is now an offence contrary to the *Indecency With Children Act 1960* where the child is under the age of 14. On the question of whether requiring a "threatening gesture or threat to use force" means that hostility is an element of indecent assault, see *R. v. McCormack* (1969) (see p. 48).

---

**KEY PRINCIPLE:** *An assault is indecent if "right minded persons would consider the conduct . . . so offensive to contemporary standards of modesty and privacy as to be indecent."*

## R. v. Court 1989

The defendant spanked a girl several times across her clothed buttocks, due to his "buttocks fetish". He appealed against conviction for indecent assault on the basis that the reason for his actions was not admissible evidence.

**HELD:** (H.L.) Appeal dismissed for reasons given below. *Obiter*, Lord Ackner indicated that indecency was a question for the jury on the test given above. Lord Griffiths also defined indecency as "conduct that right-thinking people will consider an affront to . . . sexual modesty . . .". [1989] A.C. 28

---

**KEY PRINCIPLE:** *If an assault is not objectively capable of being regarded as indecent, a defendant's undisclosed indecent motive cannot render it indecent.*

## R. v. George 1956

The defendant attempted to remove a woman's shoe because he obtained sexual gratification from doing so.

**HELD:** Since there were no overt circumstances of indecency towards the person assaulted, the defendant could not be guilty of indecent assault and his indecent motive was irrelevant. The defendant was guilty common assault. [1956] Crim. L.R. 52

### COMMENTARY

The case was approved in *R. v. Court* (1989) (see p. 52). A similar case is *R. v. Thomas* (1985) where a school caretaker was not guilty of indecent assault in rubbing the bottom of a 12-year old girl's skirt because the conduct was not capable of being indecent whatever his motive.

**KEY PRINCIPLE:** *If an assault is not inherently indecent but is objectively capable of being regarded as indecent, a defendant's motive or intention is admissible to determine whether or not it actually was indecent.*

## R. v. Court 1989

(see p. 47).

**HELD:** (H.L.) Appeal dismissed. The defendant's conduct was capable of being regarded as indecent. In order to decide whether or not it actually was indecent, a jury needed to consider all the circumstances (including the relationship of defendant to victim and both how and why the assault occurred). Therefore, the defendant's explanation of the reasons for the assault was admissible to establish whether or not the conduct was indecent. [1989] A.C. 28

### COMMENTARY
Objectively, the defendant's conduct was not inherently indecent (*i.e.* it was equivocal) but it was capable of being regarded as indecent. This distinguished *George*. Presumably, the distinction rests on what a hypothetical bystander, without knowledge of the defendant's motives, would think of the conduct. If s/he would think it was not indecent, motive cannot make it indecent (*George* and *Thomas*). If s/he would be unsure whether it was indecent or not (as in *Court*), motive is admissible to determine the issue.

---

**KEY PRINCIPLE:** *Lack of consent is generally required for indecent assault but victims under the age of 16 cannot, in law, consent to the offence.*

## R. v. McCormack 1969

The defendant was acquitted of unlawful sexual intercourse with an under aged girl, but convicted of indecently assaulting the 15-year old who consented to the sexual contact.

**HELD:** (D.C.) Appeal dismissed. The girl was under 16 and so her consent was no defence under *Sexual Offences Act 1956*, s.14(2). [1969] 2 Q.B. 442

### COMMENTARY
This case also confirms that *Sexual Offences Act 1956*, s.6 (under-age sex) includes an allegation of indecent assault.

Therefore a defendant might be found guilty of indecent assault although he is acquitted of s.6 because no sexual intercourse took place or because he has the s.6(3) ("young man's") defence.

**KEY PRINCIPLE:** *Hostility is not a requirement additional to lack of consent in indecent assault.*

## R. v. McCormack 1969

(see p. 48).

**HELD:** (D.C.) Since the girl was under 16, her consent was no defence and it was therefore irrelevant that there was no compulsion or hostility from the defendant. [1969] 2 Q.B. 442

**COMMENTARY**
The case dispels doubt by following *Faulkner v. Talbot* (1981) where it was said that an indecent assault need "not necessarily be hostile or rude or aggressive, as some of the cases seem to indicate." This received further approval in *Thomas* and *Court*.

**KEY PRINCIPLE:** *Where an indecent assault is intended or objectively likely to cause bodily harm (of a non-transitory and non-trifling nature), consent is no defence.*

## R. v. Boyea 1992

The defendant was convicted of indecent assault by engaging in conduct causing injuries consistent with force being used.

**HELD:** (C.A.) Defendant's appeal dismissed. Where actual bodily harm was intended or likely, consent was no defence to indecent assault. [1992] Crim. L.R. 574.

**COMMENTARY**
Following *Boyea*, even where injury is not intended or foreseen, consensual sexual activity amounts to indecent assault if bodily harm was likely. This and similar cases appear in Chapter 4.

**KEY PRINCIPLE:** *In determining whether an injury is such that consent is irrelevant, consideration is given to current* *social attitudes regarding acceptable degrees of injury occurring in sexual activities.*

## R. v. Boyea 1992

(see p. 49).

**HELD:** (C.A.) Consent is irrelevant if the injury is not transitory or trifling. The definition of these terms rests on modern standards of acceptable behaviour in sexual contact. It is possible that people can now consent to a greater level of injury than in the past because it would now be regarded as transitory or trifling. [1992] Crim.L.R. 574

---

**KEY PRINCIPLE:** *There is no equivalent to the marital rape exemption for sexual acts (other than sexual intercourse).*

## R. v. Kowalski 1988

The defendant forced his estranged wife to engage in fellatio. He pleaded guilty to indecent assault following a direction that the conduct was capable of amounting to the offence.

**HELD:** (C.A.) Appeal dismissed. The marital exemption, based on implied consent, only applies to intercourse *per vaginam*. Actual consent is required if other acts (such as oral intercourse) are not to amount to indecent assault. (1988) 86 Cr. App. R. 339

### COMMENTARY

The case was decided prior to the abolition of the marital rape exemption. It confirms (overruling *Caswell* (1984)) that it is irrelevant whether the acts in question are preliminary to sexual intercourse and whether they had previously been consented to.

# Indecent Assault: The *Mens Rea*

**KEY PRINCIPLE:** *Indecent assault requires proof of intention to assault; recklessness is not sufficient.*

## R. v. Parsons 1993

The defendant was convicted of indecently assaulting his stepdaughters. He appealed against the direction that indecent assault could be committed recklessly.

**HELD:** (C.A.) Appeal allowed. Recklessness was only relevant in the context of lack of consent. The rest of the offence required proof of intention to assault in circumstances of indecency. [1993] Crim. L.R. 792

**COMMENTARY**
This follows *Court* which also appears to require intention in relation to the element of assault.

---

**KEY PRINCIPLE:** *Proof of indecent intention is a necessary element in some cases of indecent assault.*

## R. v. Pratt 1984

The defendant forced two boys to strip and expose their genitals late one night on a quayside.

**HELD:** (Cr. Ct.) Indecent intention was a necessary ingredient of the offence and so the defendant's claim that his sole motive was to search for cannabis which he thought the boys had stolen from him could be used to disprove this intent. [1984] Crim. L.R. 41

**COMMENTARY**
This case received approval in *Court*.

---

**KEY PRINCIPLE:** *Where an assault is inherently indecent, the mens rea is satisfied by proof that the defendant intended to assault in circumstances which are, in fact, indecent.*

## R. v. Court 1989

(see p. 47).

**COMMENTARY**
Lord Ackner indicated that motive is irrelevant in cases of inherently (unambiguously) indecent assaults. He gave the example of a man stripping a woman without her consent, saying that the man's purpose was not relevant since the prosecution only had to show that he intended to assault the woman in a manner which was (objectively) indecent. This suggests that it is enough that the defendant is aware of the circumstances that are indecent: indecent intention need not be proved.

---

**KEY PRINCIPLE:** *Where an assault is not inherently indecent but is capable of being indecent, it is necessary to prove that the defendant had an indecent intention.*

# R. v. Court 1989

**HELD:** (H.L.) Where, as in the current case, the conduct is not inherently indecent but could be given an innocent or indecent interpretation, the prosecution must prove that the defendant had an indecent purpose.

**COMMENTARY**
Lord Ackner's approval of *Pratt* (see p. 51) suggests that he viewed it as a case falling under this category of "ambiguous indecency" where motive/reason is crucial in determining the existence of indecency and the requisite *mens rea*. However, it is difficult to see why the conduct in *Pratt* is not "unambiguously indecent" and within the former principle instead. [1989] A.C. 28

---

**KEY PRINCIPLE:** *Subjective recklessness as to lack of consent is sufficient* mens rea *for indecent assault.*

# R. v. Kimber 1983

The defendant was convicted of indecently assaulting a female hospital patient. He appealed against the direction that belief in consent was no defence.

**HELD:** (C.A.) Appeal dismissed. The defendant's evidence established that he was indifferent to the issue of consent which was sufficient to amount to recklessness. [1983] 3 All E.R. 316

**COMMENTARY**
The case suggests that recklessness in indecent assault bears the same meaning as in rape, requiring proof that the defendant "could not care less". Objective (*Caldwell*) recklessness is not sufficient for the offence, confirmed in *Parsons* (1993) (see p. 50).

---

**KEY PRINCIPLE:** *The mens rea of indecent assault is disproved by an honest (albeit unreasonable) belief that the victim consents.*

## R. v. Kimber 1983

(see p. 52).

**HELD:** (C.A.) Following *Morgan* (1976), there had been a misdirection because honest belief in consent would disprove knowledge of or recklessness as to lack of consent. Such a belief did not have to be based on reasonable grounds. However, the defendant's appeal was dismissed because of evidence that he had not genuinely believed that the victim consented (see above). [1983] 3 All E.R. 316

# 6. HOMICIDE

## *Actus reus*

**KEY PRINCIPLE:** *The defendant must cause the death of a human being under the Queen's peace.*

## Attorney-General's Reference (No. 3 of 1994) 1996

The defendant stabbed a pregnant woman, injuring the baby which was born alive but died from the injuries sustained. The judge directed that this disclosed no case to answer.

**HELD:** (C.A.) If a child is born alive, with existence independent of its mother, homicide can be charged in respect of injuries inflicted on a child or mother that then cause its death. [1996] Crim L.R. 268, C.A.

### COMMENTARY
(1) The position differs if the child is miscarried or still born.
(2) For the principles relating to factual and legal causation, see Chapter 1.
(3) The old principle that death must occur within a year and a day of any injury has been abolished by the *Law Reform (Year and a Day Rule) Act 1996*. However, the consent of the Attorney-General is required for any case where more than three years has elapsed between the death and the injury (or where the defendant has already been convicted of an offence in respect of the activity).

# Murder—*Mens Rea*

**KEY PRINCIPLE:** *Murder requires proof of intention to kill or intention to cause grievous bodily harm.*

## R. v. Moloney 1985
(see Chapter 2, p. 15).

**HELD:** (H.L.) Malice aforethought (the *mens rea* of murder) is only established by proof of intention to kill or cause grievous bodily harm. Recklessness is not sufficient. [1985] A.C. 905

---

**KEY PRINCIPLE:** *Intention to kill or cause grievous bodily harm can be inferred from evidence that the defendant foresaw death or grievous bodily harm as a natural and probable (virtually certain) consequence.*

## R. v. Moloney 1985

## R. v. Hancock & Shankland 1986

## R. v. Nedrick 1986

**COMMENTARY**
Discussed in Chapter 2.

# Voluntary Manslaughter: Diminished Responsibility

**KEY PRINCIPLE:** *The defendant must prove an "abnormality of mind" which covers all aspects of the mind's activities, including the ability to control impulses or urges.*

## R. v. Byrne 1960
A sexual psychopath pleaded diminished responsibility, having killed a woman whilst suffering from violent sexual desires which he could not resist or had difficulty resisting. The judge ruled that such impulses or urges did not fall within the defence.

**HELD:** (C.A.) Defendant's appeal allowed, manslaughter substituted. Abnormality of mind was "a state of mind so different from that of ordinary human beings that the reasonable man would term it abnormal". There had been a misdirection because this covered not only "perception of physical acts" and "ability to form a rational judgement as to . . . right or wrong" but also "the ability to exercise will-power to control physical acts". [1960] 2 Q.B. 396

## COMMENTARY

The court contrasted "abnormality of mind" with the "defect of reason" required in insanity. "Abnormality of mind" was also described in *R. v. Thornton* (1992) (see p. 58) as covering "capacity to understand", "ability to make sensible, rational judgments" and "ability . . . to exercise control".

---

**KEY PRINCIPLE:** *The abnormality of mind must arise from "arrested or retarded development of mind or any inherent causes or induced by disease or injury." (Homicide Act 1957, s.2)*

**KEY PRINCIPLE:** *Where the abnormality may have been caused by a number of factors, the jury should consider diminished responsibility by reference only to factors falling within section 2.*

## R. v. Gittens 1984

The defendant, who suffered from depression, had been drinking and taking prescribed drugs when he killed his wife and step-daughter. He was convicted of murder and appealed against the direction on diminished responsibility.

**HELD:** (C.A.) Appeal allowed, manslaughter substituted. Where there is a combination of causes of the abnormality, the jury must disregard the effect of matters (like intoxication) that fall outside section 2, and should only consider the effect of matters (like depression) that fall within section 2. [1984] 1 Q.B.698

---

**KEY PRINCIPLE:** *The abnormality must substantially impair mental responsibility, which is a question for the jury to decide.*

## R. v. Byrne 1960

(see p. 55).

**COMMENTARY**

The court suggested that "substantial impairment" might equate, in ordinary language, with "partial insanity" or "on the border-line of insanity". This is criticised in the next case.

---

**KEY PRINCIPLE:** *The impairment of responsibility need not be total but must be more than trivial.*

## R. v. Seers 1984

The defendant killed his wife whilst suffering from chronic depression. He was convicted of murder following a direction that the test for diminished responsibility was whether he was "partially insane or on the borderline of insanity".

**HELD:** (C.A.) Defendant's appeal allowed, manslaughter substituted because of a misleading direction. There was sufficient evidence that responsibility had been "seriously" (more than trivially) and therefore substantially impaired. (1984) 79 Cr. App. R. 261

**COMMENTARY**

The case disapproves the "partial insanity" test suggested in *Byrne. Thornton* (see p. 58) confirms that "substantial" means "more than mere trivial . . . but . . . not . . . total or absolute impairment."

# Voluntary Manslaughter: Provocation

**KEY PRINCIPLE:** *Things done and/or said are capable of providing evidence of provocation if they cause the defendant to lose self-control.*

## R. v. Doughty 1986

The defendant was charged with murdering his 17-day old baby, having lost his temper due to the baby's persistent crying. The judge ruled that "natural episodes or events such as the baby crying could not be evidence of provocation."

**HELD:** (C.A.) Defendant's appeal allowed, manslaughter substituted. Under section 3 of the *Homicide Act 1957*, provocation was no longer limited to unlawful or wrongful acts. The crying may have caused the defendant's response and so provocation should have been left to the jury. (1986) 83 Cr. App. R. 319

**COMMENTARY**
Under s.3, most things causing loss of control are capable of being provocation. This includes self-induced provocation: *R. v. Johnson* (1989) (see below). Moreover, provocation no longer has to come from the victim nor be aimed at the defendant.

---

**KEY PRINCIPLE:** *If there is evidence of provocation, the judge has a duty to leave the issue to the jury even where the defendant does not raise the defence.*

## R. v. Johnson 1989

The defendant behaved in a threatening manner which caused the victim to attack him. The defendant stabbed and killed the victim and pleaded self-defence but not provocation. He was convicted of murder and appealed that, in the light of the evidence, the judge should have directed on provocation.

**HELD:** (C.A.) Appeal allowed, manslaughter substituted. The jury rejected self-defence and so could have inferred loss of self-control from the evidence. Therefore the judge had a duty to leave the issue to the jury. [1989] 2 All E.R. 839

**COMMENTARY**
This is also why provocation should have been left to the jury in *Doughty* and *Baille* (1995). It has since been confirmed that not only must judges direct on provocation but also both counsel have a duty to request such a direction: *R. v. Cox* (1995).

---

**KEY PRINCIPLE:** *To establish provocation in fact, the defendant must suffer a sudden and temporary loss of self-control at the time of the killing.*

## R. v. Thornton 1992

The defendant, who had a personality disorder, killed her husband after a history of abuse. They argued and she went to the kitchen, sharpened a knife, and returned to where he lay. He threatened to kill her when she was asleep and she stabbed him. She raised diminished responsibility and the judge also directed on provocation.

**HELD:** (C.A.) Defendant's appeal against conviction for murder dismissed.

(1) The direction on diminished responsibility) was accurate.

(2) There was no misdirection on provocation. Devlin J.'s statement in *R v. Duffy* (1949) that provocation required proof of a "sudden and temporary loss of self-control" was still correct. The defendant, having gone to the kitchen, had time to reflect, "had cooled down" and regained self-control. [1992] 1 All E.R. 306

**COMMENTARY**
The court maintained that "sudden loss of control" was still appropriate test even where there had been a history of provocation, including domestic violence. This was raised again in *R. v. Ahluwalia* (1992) (see p. 59) and confirmed in Thornton;s subsequent appeal in 1996. This appeal was based on fresh medical evidence of Thornton's personality disorder and battered woman's syndrome. The Court of Appeal held that this new evidence might be relevant to her defence (see below) and that subsequent case law might mean that her conviction was unsafe and unsatisfactory. Her conviction was quashed and a retrial ordered which subsequently led to a finding of manslaughter.

---

**KEY PRINCIPLE:** *The longer the "cooling period" between the provocation and the killing, the less likely that the defence will succeed.*

# R. v. Ibrahms & Gregory 1982

The defendants had been terrorised by the victim for some time and carried out their plan to kill him five days after the last act of provocation. They were convicted of murder after the judge withdrew provocation from the jury.

**HELD:** (C.A.) Defendant's appeal dismissed. The substantial time lapse between the provocation and the killing, the fact that there was no provoking act just before the killing, and the formation of the plan presented no evidence of loss of self-control at the relevant time. (1982) 74 Cr. App. R 154

**COMMENTARY**
The court approved *Duffy* that a "desire for revenge", "time to think, to reflect" suggested no sudden loss of control. However this does not automatically negate provocation; they are simply factors for the jury to consider when deciding the issue: *Ahluwalia*.

## R. v. Ahluwalia 1992

The defendant killed her husband after years of abuse and violence. He threatened her and when he fell asleep she threw petrol into his room and set fire to it. Charged with murder, she pleaded lack of intent and provocation as alternatives. She was convicted and appealed against the direction on provocation and also because of fresh evidence of diminished responsibility.

**HELD:** (C.A.) Retrial ordered to consider the evidence of diminished responsibility. The direction on provocation had made it clear that the lack of immediate response did not necessarily disprove the defence but was merely one factor for the jury to take into account. [1992] 4 All E.R. 889

**COMMENTARY**
In line with *Thornton* and *Ibrahms*, the court indicated that the longer the time lapse, the less likely the defence would succeed, but this was ultimately a question for the jury. A similar decision was reached in *R. v. Baille* 1995. In *Ahluwalia* the court refused to consider the argument that in domestic violence cases, a time lapse could create a slow-burn reaction rather than an immediate loss of control. Any change in the law was for Parliament not the courts.

---

**KEY PRINCIPLE:** *The jury must consider all the circumstances in deciding whether the defendant lost self-control.*

## R. v. Humphries 1995

The defendant had been abused for years by the victim. The victim taunted her about a repeated suicide attempt and caused her to think that he was going to rape her just before she killed him. She was convicted of murder.

**HELD:** (C.A.) Defendant's appeal allowed, manslaughter substituted. The judge should have directed the jury to consider the various strands of "cumulative" provocation when assessing "loss of control". The defendant's characteristics were also relevant to this issue. [1995] 4 All E.R. 1008

## COMMENTARY

(1) This confirms the approach towards cumulative provocation. In deciding on loss of control the jury must consider "the whole picture, the whole story": *Ahluwalia, Thornton.*
(2) Factors for a jury to consider therefore include time lapses; any characteristics that may affect the defendant's self-control (see also *R. v. Morhall* (1995)); cumulative provocation; and the effect that provocation aimed at others might have on a defendant (see, for example, *R v. Pearson* (1992))

---

**KEY PRINCIPLE:** *The jury must decide whether the provocation was enough to make a reasonable person, with the defendant's characteristics, lose self-control and do as the defendant did.*

## Director of Public Prosecutions v. Camplin 1978

A 15-year old boy, lost self-control and killed the victim who had sexually assaulted and taunted him. The boy was convicted of murder on a direction that, in deciding whether the reasonable person would have lost control and done as he did, the test was simply the reaction of a reasonable adult. The defendant's appeal was allowed on the basis that the test was that of the reasonable person of the same age as the defendant. The D.P.P. appealed.

**HELD:** (H.L.) Appeal dismissed. Lord Diplock gave the following direction: "the reasonable man . . . is a person having the same power of self-control to be expected of an ordinary person of the sex and age of the accused, but in other respects sharing such of the accused characteristics as they think would affect the gravity of the provocation to him; and the question is not merely whether such a person would in like circumstances be provoked to lose his self-control but also whether he would react . . . as the accused did." [1978] A.C. 705

**COMMENTARY**

(1) The case overrules *Bedder v. D.P.P.* (1954) (which imposed a purely objective test) and *Mancini v. D.P.P.* (1942) (on the requirement of proportionality between the gravity of the provocation and the response of the defendant).

(2) The court excluded from the test characteristics such as exceptional excitability, pugnaciousness, bad temper or intoxication. The particular characteristics in question in the case were sex and age. Other characteristics that the court thought might be relevant included: race; colour; ethnicity; physical infirmity and disability; being impotent or pregnant; and having a shameful incident in one's past.

(3) The decision implies that age is always relevant and many cases do impute the defendant's age to the reasonable person (including mental age as in *R. v. Raven* (1982)). However, *R. v. Ali* (1989) held that it was unnecessary to allude to the defendant's age (20) because there would be no difference in the response of a reasonable 20-year old and that of a person of any other age to the type of provocation in question.

---

**KEY PRINCIPLE:** *For particular characteristics to be considered, they must be sufficiently permanent and the provocation must relate to them.*

# R. v. Newell 1980

A chronic alcoholic was grief-stricken by the recent desertion of his girlfriend and was drinking heavily with a friend. The friend made an insensitive remark about the girlfriend and suggested a homosexual encounter. This caused the defendant to lose self-control and kill the friend. He was convicted of murder and appealed against the direction on provocation (given before the decision in *Camplin*).

**HELD:** (C.A.) Appeal dismissed. The judge's direction would not have been affected by *Camplin*. Not every trait was imputed to the reasonable man. Intoxication and grief at the loss of his girlfriend were not characteristics because they were transitory. The only thing with sufficient permanence to be a characteristic was chronic alcoholism. However, the provoking words had no connection with the alcoholism and so it was not a relevant characteristic. (1980) 71 Cr. App. R. 331

**COMMENTARY**

(1) Transitory states of mind such as depression, excitability, irascibility or intoxication are not characteristics. Whilst temporary depression is not relevant, post-traumatic stress disorder or battered women's syndrome can be relevant, if sufficiently permanent see *Ahluwalia* and *Thornton* (1996). Moreover, whilst mere intoxication is not relevant, a sufficiently permanent addiction might be if (unlike *Newell*) the defendant is provoked about it. In *R. v. Morhall* (1995) the defendant was provoked about his addiction to solvent abuse. The addiction was held to relevant not only to the question of loss of control but also as a characteristic in the reasonable person test.

(2) Difficulties might arise with mental peculiarities because of the requirement that there be acts or words directed at the characteristic. This was not problematic in *Raven* (see p. 61) because the court treated low mental age as equivalent to physical age. Moreover, in *Humphries* (see p. 60), the taunting about the suicide attempts enabled the defendant's immature, attention-seeking behaviour to be taken into account.

# Involuntary Manslaughter: Constructive Liability

**KEY PRINCIPLE:** *The defendant must commit the actus reus and have any mens rea required for the unlawful act which causes the death.*

## R. v. Lamb 1967

The defendant was convicted of manslaughter, having shot and killed a friend. Misunderstanding how the gun worked, neither the defendant nor the victim anticipated injury.

**HELD:** (C.A.) Defendant's appeal allowed due to a misdirection. There was no unlawful act (assault) without proof of the *actus reus* and *mens rea*. Since the latter was missing, the offence was incomplete. [1967] 2 Q.B. 981

## COMMENTARY

(1) There was no *actus reus* of psychic assault because the victim did not apprehend contact, nor was there physical assault because of lack of *mens rea*. For further examples, see *Slingsby* (see Chapter 4) where there was no assault because of consent and *R. v. Scarlett* (1993) (see Chapter 14, p. 159) where there was no assault because the force was used in defence of property.

(2) In *R v. Cato* (1976) (see p. 65) stating, *obiter*, that the unlawful act could be possession of heroin, the court appeared to overlook the requirement that the unlawful act cause the death since it was administration and not possession that caused the death. A similar point is raised in *R v. Dalby* (1982) where death was caused by self-adminstration of a drug unlawfully supplied by the defendant. The court stated that the supply in itself was not an act which caused direct harm.

---

**KEY PRINCIPLE:** *The unlawful act must also be dangerous, in the sense that the reasonable person would realise that it creates a risk of some physical harm, albeit slight.*

# R v. Church 1966
(see Chapter 1, p. 13).

**HELD:** (C.A.) Defendant's appeal dismissed. In the context of constructive manslaughter, the "unlawful act must be such as all sober and reasonable people would inevitably recognise must subject the other person to, at least, the risk of some harm . . . albeit not serious harm." [1966] 1 Q.B. 59

## COMMENTARY

*R. v. Dawson* (1985) confirms that the harm foreseen by the reasonable person must be physical and not merely mental. The defendants had committed a robbery at a garage, using, *inter alia*, a replica gun. The 60-year old attendant suffered from heart disease and died as a result. It was held to be a misdirection to suggest that emotional disturbance was sufficient for the act to be "dangerous". See also *R. v. Watson* (1989), which decides that the reasonable person is endowed with any knowledge of the circumstances that the defendant gains in the course of the unlawful act. On the facts, this included knowledge of the victim's age and physical condition.

---

**KEY PRINCIPLE:** *The defendant must intend to do the unlawful act but it is not necessary to show that s/he intended or foresaw any harm.*

## D.P.P. v. Newbury & Jones 1977

The defendants caused the death of a train guard by pushing a paving stone from a parapet onto a train. They were convicted of manslaughter on a direction that it was not necessary to show that they foresaw harm to a person.

**HELD:** (H.L.) Defendant's appeal dismissed. Constructive manslaughter requires that the defendant intentionally did the act which is unlawful and dangerous. It is not necessary to prove that s/he knew that it was unlawful or dangerous. Moreover, following *Church*, the test for "dangerous act" is objective. [1977] A.C. 500

### COMMENTARY

It was held in *R. v. Dalby* (1982) that the unlawful act "must be an act directed at the victim and likely to cause immediate injury, however slight". This was originally interpreted as requiring proof that the defendant intended to direct the act at a person. However, this view was rejected in *R. v. Goodfellow* (1986) where it was decided that it was sufficient that the defendant intentionally committed an act which was unlawful and caused death. Thus, arson was a sufficiently unlawful act in the case.

# Involuntary Manslaughter: Recklessness and Gross Negligence

**KEY PRINCIPLE:** *Where liability is not based on an unlawful act, the prosecution must prove recklessness or gross negligence*

# R. v. Cato 1976

The defendant caused the death of a friend by administering heroin to him with consent.

**HELD:** (C.A.) Manslaughter by recklessness or gross negligence was an alternative to manslaughter based on an unlawful act. [1976] 1 All E.R. 260

### COMMENTARY

Recklessness was described in the case as a "perfectly simple English word". In *Goodfellow*, the court referred to the subjective element of recklessness in manslaughter ("appreciating a risk"). However, there is some doubt as to the nature of risk to be foreseen. Certainly foresight of death (or grievous bodily harm) should be sufficient but so too might foresight of less serious physical injury. *Goodfellow* also applied the *Lawrence* direction on recklessness to manslaughter but this approach is rejected in the next case.

# R. v. Adomako 1994

An anaesthetist failed to notice that a tube supplying oxygen to a patient had become disconnected during an operation. The patient died as a result. He was convicted of manslaughter and appealed.

**HELD:** (H.L.) In such cases, it is necessary to prove that the breach of a duty of care caused the death and that, in all the circumstances, the breach was so grossly negligent as to be characterised as criminal. [1994] 3 All E.R. 79

### COMMENTARY

The court referred to the risk of death to the patient that had to be involved and also decided that whilst the term "recklessness" might be used, the *Lawrence* direction on recklessness should not be used in the context of gross negligence.

# 7. THEFT

## Appropriation

**KEY PRINCIPLE:** *Appropriation is "Any assumption by a person of the rights of an owner . . . and this includes, where he has come by the property (innocently or not) without stealing it, any later assumption of a right to it by keeping or dealing with it as owner"* Theft Act 1968, s.3(1).

**KEY PRINCIPLE:** *Appropriation is established by the assumption of any one right of an owner.*

### R. v. Morris 1984

The defendant swapped price labels on supermarket goods. On appeal against conviction for theft, the question was whether appropriation required an assumption of all of the rights of an owner or whether it was sufficient to assume just one right.

**HELD:** (H.L.) Appeal dismissed. It was sufficient to prove an assumption of any of the rights. [1984] A.C. 320.

### COMMENTARY

Acts such as touching or moving goods may therefore be appropriation. However, *obiter*, the House limited its scope by requiring that it be an unauthorised act ("an adverse interference"). This requirement has now been overturned by *D.P.P.v. Gomez* (1993) (see p. 67).

---

**KEY PRINCIPLE:** *Appropriation can occur even though the act is expressly or impliedly authorised or consented to by the owner.*

### Lawrence v. Metropolitan Police Commissioner 1972

A taxi driver overcharged a passenger (who understood little English). He falsely stated that the offered fare was insufficient and took further monies from the wallet that the passenger held open to him. He was convicted of theft and appealed on the basis that consent prevented liability.

**HELD:** (H.L.) Appeal dismissed. The facts probably did not establish consent but, in any event, the prosecution did not have to prove that the taking was without consent. [1972] A.C. 626

**COMMENTARY**
Despite various attempts at reconciliation, there seemed to be a conflict between *Lawrence* and the view in *Morris* that appropriation involves "not an act expressly or impliedly authorised by the owner". Nevertheless, in *Morris*, Lord Roskill agreed that *Lawrence* was rightly decided. He also approved *R. v. Skipp* (1975) (C.A.) where appropriation did not occur until the defendant did an unauthorised act of diverting from his delivery route and *Eddy v. Niman* (1981) (D.C.) where would-be shoplifters were not guilty of theft having done no more than put goods into shop trolleys (authorised acts). In *R. v. Fritschy* (1985) (C.A.) the court followed *Morris* but in *Dobson v. General Accident* (1990) (a civil case), the Court of Appeal followed *Lawrence*. The Court of Appeal in *Gomez* (1993) followed *Morris*, but the matter has now been resolved by the House of Lords.

---

## D.P.P. v. Gomez 1993

The defendant obtained authority for transactions by falsely representing that stolen cheques were genuine. His conviction for theft of the goods was quashed following *Morris* and the Crown appealed.

**HELD:** (H.L.) Appeal allowed. It was not possible to reconcile *Morris* and *Lawrence*. *Morris* was incorrect and *Lawrence* should be followed. Therefore the defendant was guilty because appropriation occurred despite consent. [1993] A.C. 442.

**COMMENTARY**
(1) The decision in *Morris* that the assumption of any right amounts to appropriation was approved. Combined with the fact that this can now be consensual or authorised, theft widens yet further in scope because, for example, touching goods on a shop-shelf may now be appropriation.
(2) *Skipp* and *Fritschy* were overruled, being inconsistent with *Lawrence*. Presumably, *Eddy v. Niman* is also incorrect because, following *obiter* in *Gomez*, putting goods in a shop trolley may be appropriation.
(3) Despite some statements in the case suggesting a wider

application, *Gomez* may be restricted to cases where consent is obtained by a decpetion. This was the view taken in *R. v. Mazo* (1996).

(4) Following *Gomez*, most cases of obtaining property by deception (*Theft Act 1968*, s.15) are now also cases of theft. Parliamentary creation of a separate offence (section 15) to deal with "consensual" parting with property induced by deception is a strong argument against the decision. For an example of the overlap operating in favour of a defendant, see *R. v. Atakpu* (1993) (see below).

(5) The courts have experienced difficulty in applying *Gomez*. See, for example, *R. v. Gallasso* (1994) and *R. v. Mazo* (1996)

---

**KEY PRINCIPLE:** *If property is stolen once, it cannot be appropriated again by the same person exercising rights over it.*

## R. v. Atakpu 1993

The defendants hired vehicles abroad by deception and delivered them to Dover, intending to ring and sell them in England. They were convicted of conspiracy to steal (which required proof that the cars were stolen in England).

**HELD:** (C.A.) Defendant's appeal allowed. By virtue of *Gomez* (H.L.), the obtaining of the cars abroad by deception was also theft. Since it was not possible for the stolen cars to be stolen again by the same thieves, there was no theft in England. [1993] 4 All E.R. 215

### COMMENTARY

*Theft Act 1968*, s.3 says that a later assumption amounts to appropriation where the person has "come by the property . . . without stealing it". This precluded the possibility of appropriation by the same person's later assumption of property already acquired by theft. The court also noted that *R. v. Hircock* (1978) was no longer good law in the light of *Gomez*. In *Hircock*, it was held that the hiring of a car by deception was not theft, so that selling the car thereafter could be theft.

---

**KEY PRINCIPLE:** *Appropriation can be a continuous act but only for as long as the defendant is acting in the course of the same transaction.*

## R. v. Atakpu 1993

(see p. 68).

**HELD:** (C.A.) The second ground for allowing the appeal was that the theft abroad did not continue in England (by retention after the hire period or by ringing the cars). The court agreed that appropriation can occur instantaneously (*R. v. Pitham & Hehl* (1976) see below and Chapter 9, p. 102) or it can continue for as long as "the thief can sensibly be regarded as in the act of stealing" (*R. v. Hale* (1978), see Chapter 9, p. 94). However, it could not be said that theft of the cars continued for days after they had first been taken. [1993] 4 All E.R. 215

**COMMENTARY**
(see also *Lockley* (1995).)

---

**KEY PRINCIPLE:** *Appropriation can occur without coming into possession or contact with the property.*

## R. v. Pitham & Hehl 1976

The two defendants bought furniture from M (to whom it did not belong) and arrived to collect it. They were convicted of handling stolen goods and appealed. The question turned on whether M had stolen the furniture before the defendants "handled".

**HELD:** (C.A.) Appeal dismissed. M assumed the rights of an owner by inviting the defendants to buy the furniture. The appropriation was complete on the offer to sell and so the defendants had handled stolen goods. (1976) 65 Cr. App. R.45.

**COMMENTARY**
Another example of appropriation without contact with the property is *Ex p. Osman* (1990).

# Property

**KEY PRINCIPLE:** *"'Property' includes money and all other property, real or personal, including things in action and other intangible property."* Theft Act 1968, *s.4.*

**KEY PRINCIPLE:** *"Money" in a bank account in credit or within an overdraft facility is a "thing in action", capable of being stolen.*

## R. v. Kohn 1979

An accountant used company cheques to draw money from company bank accounts for himself. In some transactions the account was in credit. In others, it was in overdraft within an overdraft facility limit. In others, it was in overdraft in excess of the limit. The defendant appealed against conviction for theft of the cheques and from the accounts.

**HELD:** (C.A.) Appeal dismissed in respect of stealing from the accounts in credit and those within an overdraft facility. Where an account is in credit, the debt owed by the bank to the customer is a thing in action. A bank is also obliged to meet a cheque drawn on an account within its overdraft facility. This obligation is also a thing in action, capable of being stolen. (1979) 69 Cr. App. R. 395.

**COMMENTARY**

The court said that appropriation did not occur "until the transaction has gone through to completion". However, since *Morris* and *Gomez*, the offence can occur earlier by simply drawing or presenting a cheque. This is confirmed in *ex p. Osman* (1990) where sending a telex, instructing a bank to pay money from one account into another was appropriation of the debt.

---

**KEY PRINCIPLE:** *There is no property, capable of being appropriated, where a bank account if overdrawn without (or in excess of) an overdraft facility.*

## R. v. Kohn 1979

(see above).

**HELD:** (C.A.) Appeal allowed in respect of stealing from the accounts overdrawn beyond the agreed overdraft limit. No relationship of debtor/creditor arose and the bank had no obligation to meet cheques drawn on these accounts. Therefore there was no thing in action, capable of being stolen. (1979) 69 Cr. App. R.395.

## R. v. Navvabi 1986

The defendant used cheque cards, obliging a bank to honour cheques when there were insufficient funds in the account and no overdraft facility. He was convicted of theft from the bank.

**HELD:** (C.A.) Defendant's appeal allowed. There was no appropriation of identifiable property in which the bank had rights. By using the card, the defendant had done nothing that assumed any rights of the bank to part of its funds. [1986] 3 All E.R 102.

### COMMENTARY

The defendant should have been charged with obtaining a pecuniary advantage (see Chapter 9).

---

**KEY PRINCIPLE:** *A cheque is two separate types of property capable of being stolen: a piece of paper and a thing of action.*

## R. v. Duru 1973

The defendants were charged with obtaining property (cheques) belonging to the G.L.C. by deception (false mortgage application details). They appealed against conviction for reasons discussed below and in Chapter 8.

**HELD:** (C.A.) Dismissing the appeal, it was established that the cheques were pieces of paper (the cheque form—personal property) and the money represented by the cheque (a thing in action—a legal right to sue on the cheque). [1973] 3 All E.R. 715.

### COMMENTARY

Following *Duru*, the appeal in *Kohn* (see p. 70) was also dismissed in respect of stealing the cheques.

---

**KEY PRINCIPLE:** *Confidential information is not property capable of being stolen.*

## Oxford v. Moss 1978

A student "borrowed" an examination paper to obtain advanced knowledge of the questions. He was charged with stealing the confidential information (the exam questions) and acquitted on the basis that this was not property capable of being stolen.

**HELD:** (D.C.) Prosecution appeal dismissed. Confidence is a right over property but not a form of intangible property for the purposes of theft. (1978) 68 Cr. App. R 183

**COMMENTARY**
Some forms of intellectual property do fall within s4 either as "intangible property" (*e.g.* a patent) or as a "thing in action" (*e.g.* a copyright or trade mark). However, by analogy with *Oxford v. Moss*, a trade secret is not property.

# Belonging to Another

**KEY PRINCIPLE:** *Property belongs "to any person having possession or control . . . or . . . any proprietary right or interest . . ."* Theft Act 1968, *s.5(1).*

**KEY PRINCIPLE:** *Control of land may include control of articles on the land.*

## R. v. Woodman 1974
The defendants were convicted of stealing scrap metal from a disused site owned by E.C.C. The site was surrounded by barbed wire and notices, declaring it to be private property and excluding trespassers.

**HELD:** (C.A.) Defendant's appeal dismissed. E.C.C. demonstrated their control of the site by the steps taken to exclude others and were therefore also in control of articles on the site (whether or not they knew of their existence). [1974] 1 Q.B. 754

---

**KEY PRINCIPLE:** *A person with a proprietary right or interest can steal the property from another with possession or control.*

## R. v. Turner (No 2) 1971
The defendant took his car from a garage without paying for repairs. He was convicted of stealing the car and appealed.

**HELD:** (C.A.) Appeal dismissed. The trial judge had been correct that, even in the absence of a lien over the car, the garage owner had possession and control of it so it could be stolen from him. [1971] 2 All E.R. 441

**COMMENTARY**

This has been criticised. Whilst the repairer's lien would give the garage a proprietary right over the car, possession or control did not, in civil law, give the garage a better right to the car than the bailor (*Turner*) who could retake the goods at any time. Compare *R. v. Meredith* (1973) (no theft on removing a lawfully impounded car from police possession).

---

**KEY PRINCIPLE:** *Property may belong to someone with an equitable right or interest (other than one "arising only from an agreement to transfer or grant an interest").*

## R. v. Shadrokh-Cigari 1988

The defendant used bank drafts drawn on money credited to an account by mistake. He was convicted of theft and appealed on the basis that the drafts belonged to him and not the bank.

**HELD:** (C.A.) Appeal dismissed. Applying *Chase Manhattan Bank v. Israel-British Bank* (1981), a person paying money under mistake of fact retained an equitable interest in the money. Therefore, whilst the defendant had legal ownership of the drafts, the bank retained an equitable interest. The court also referred to section 5(4) (below) as an alternative method for reaching the same decision. [1988] Crim. L.R.465

**COMMENTARY**

The equitable interest arising in *Shadrokh* is, presumably, because the law imposes a constructive trust and so the decision in *Attorney-General's Reference* (*No. 1 of 1985*) (see p. 75) may now be doubted.

---

**KEY PRINCIPLE:** *Generally, if possession, control and the proprietary right and interest in goods pass to the defendant before the appropriation, the property does not belong to another.*

## Dip Kaur v. C.C. for Hampshire 1981

The defendant was convicted of theft of a pair of shoes. She took a pair which she knew cost £6.99 to the cashier. One was priced at £4.99, the other at £6.99 and the cashier charged £4.99 which the defendant paid.

**HELD:** (D.C.) Defendant's appeal allowed. Appropriation occurred when she took the shoes from the cashier, having paid the price charged. However, the cashier had acted within her authority and the mistake (which was not about the nature of the goods or identity of the buyer) was not fundamental and so only rendered the contract voidable. Therefore property passed under the contract and the shoes belonged to the defendant when she left the shop. [1981] 2 All.E.R.430

## COMMENTARY

(1) The court stated that section 5(4) (below) was inapplicable because, under a voidable contract, the defendant was under no obligation to restore the shoes unless or until the contract was avoided.

(2) If the mistake had been fundamental the contract would have been void and property would not have passed.

(3) Under *Gomez*, the defendant would probably be guilty because appropriation would occur earlier, whilst the shoes still belonged to the shop.

(4) For other examples of the importance in the timing of property passing see *Edwards v. Ddin* (1976) and *R. v. McHugh* (1976) (petrol put into a car); and *Corcoran v. Whent* (1977) (eating a meal in a restaurant).

---

**KEY PRINCIPLE:** *Property belongs to another under* Theft Act 1968, *s.5(3) "where a person receives property from or on account of another, and is under an obligation to the other to retain and deal with that property or its proceeds in a particular way."*

**KEY PRINCIPLE:** *Under section 5(3), there must be an arrangement giving rise to an obligation to deal with the specific property (or its proceeds) in a particular way.*

## R. v. Hall 1973

A travel agent was convicted of theft of monies received for flights. He paid the money into the firm's account but did not arrange flights and could not refund the money.

**HELD:** (C.A.) Defendant's appeal allowed. The defendant was under a contractual obligation to book and pay for flights but there was no "special arrangement" that he retain or deal with that money (or its proceeds) in that particular way. Therefore, there was no obligation to do so and the money did not belong to another under section 5(3). [1973] 1 Q.B.126

**COMMENTARY**

A similar conclusion was reached in *D.P.P. v. Huskinson* (1988) (receipt of housing benefit payments) and *Lewis v. Lethbridge* (1987) (receipt of sponsorship money). However, contrast *Wakeman v. Farrar* (1974) where, on receipt of a duplicate D.H.S.S. Giro, the defendant was under an obligation, created by written agreement, to return the original if found; and *R. v. Wain* (1993) where money (or its proceeds) collected for the Telethon Trust, paid into a special bank account, was subject to a trust obligation to be dealt with in a particular way. Note also that the obligation must be legally enforceable.

---

**KEY PRINCIPLE:** *Under section 5(3), the property must be received from or on account of another.*

# Attorney-General's Reference (No. 1 of 1985) 1986

A manager of a public house had a contract with a brewery only to sell their goods and to pay the takings into their account. He bought beer from elsewhere to make a secret profit.

**HELD:** (C.A.) The profits were not received "on account of" the brewers. Whilst the defendant had breached his contract and was under an obligation to account *to* the brewers for the profit he had not received *it on* their account. [1986] 1 Q.B. 491

**COMMENTARY**

Note the comment on this case at p. 73. It might now be possible to argue that the situation gives rise to a constructive trust (which, even if, as stated in the case, does not fall within s.5(1) does mean that the profit is obtained "on account" of the beneficiary). Support is drawn from a civil case, *Attorney-General Reference for Hong Kong v. Reid* (1994) which holds that a person in a fiduciary position, receiving a bribe, holds the bribe on constructive trust. This would also affect *Powell v. MacRae* (1977) which held that a bribe was not received "on account of" an employer.

---

**KEY PRINCIPLE:** *Property belongs to another under* Theft Act 1968, s.5(4) *if received "by another's mistake" where the recipient is "under an obligation to make restoration (in whole or part) of the property or its proceeds or of the value there of . . ."*

**KEY PRINCIPLE:** *For section 5(4), there must be an obligation to make restoration.*

## Attorney-General's Reference (No. 1 of 1983) 1985

A policewoman's bank account was mistakenly credited by direct debit with wages that she was not entitled to.

**HELD:** (C.A.) Whilst the policewoman was not under an obligation to restore the thing in action, she was under an obligation to restore its value to her employers. Therefore failure to do so could amount to theft. [1985] 1 Q.B.182

### COMMENTARY
Contrast *Dip Kaur* (see p. 73). The obligation arose here under the civil law of restitution (unjust enrichment) due to the employer's mistake. A similar decision was reached in *R. v. Davis* (1988) regarding the mistaken payment of a duplicate housing benefit cheque. *Chase Manhattan Bank* (1981) and *Shadrokh-Cigari* (1988) (see p. 73) may now render the use of section 5(4) unnecessary in these cases because the payer may retain an equitable interest so that section 5(1) applies. Certainly where a mistake is fundamental, rendering a contract void, there is no need for section 5(4).

---

**KEY PRINCIPLE:** *Under section 5(4), the obligation must be legally enforceable.*

## R. v. Gilks 1972

The defendant was convicted of theft, having refused to return money mistakenly paid to him by a bookmaker.

**HELD:** (C.A.) Defendant's appeal dismissed. The money did not belong to another by virtue of section 5(4) because a gaming transaction is not legally enforceable and so the defendant was under no obligation to repay the money. However, because of the mistake, ownership of the money never passed to the defendant and so it belonged to another under section 5(1). [1972] 3 All E.R.280

**COMMENTARY**
The ground on which the appeal was dismissed has been criticised as incorrect.

# Intention of Permanently Depriving

**KEY PRINCIPLE:** *Intention to permanently deprive is established if the defendant does not intend to return the specific property in question.*

## R. v. Velumyl 1989

The defendant took cash from his employer's safe, intending to repay the sum borrowed. He was convicted of theft.

**HELD:** (C.A.) Defendant's appeal dismissed. Intention to return objects of equivalent value might affect the issue of dishonesty but it established intention to permanently deprive of the original objects (the actual currency) taken. [1989] Crim. L.R. 299

---

**KEY PRINCIPLE:** *Under the* Theft Act 1968, *s.6(1) intent is present (even without intent to cause permanent loss of the thing) if the intent is "to treat the thing" as one's own "to dispose of regardless of the other's rights".*

## D.P.P. v. Lavender 1994

The defendant used doors from council property to replace doors in another property, belonging to the same council.

**HELD:** (D.C.) The defendant had stolen the doors. His intention was to dispose of (deal with) the property regardless of the council's rights. He had therefore intended to treat them as his own. [1994] Crim.L.R. 297

**COMMENTARY**
The court referred to *Chan Man-Sin v. Att.-Gen. of Hong Kong* (1988) as authority for the proposition that "to dispose of" included "dealing with". For an alternative view, see *R. v. Cahill* (1992) where the court accepted that it meant "to deal with definitely; to get rid of".

---

**KEY PRINCIPLE:** *Intent is established where a defendant intends to return the thing once it has ceased, in substance, to be the same thing.*

## R. v. Duru 1973

(see p. 71). One of the grounds for appeal was that there was no intent to permanently deprive the G.L.C. of the cheques.

**HELD:** (C.A.) Defendant's appeal dismissed. There was intent to permanently deprive of the cheques as things in action ("the right to receive payment"). Moreover, as a piece of paper, the cheque "changes its character completely once it is paid . . . it ceases to be in substance, the same thing as it was before." [1973] 3 All E.R. 715

### COMMENTARY

There are a number of criticisms of this reasoning, particularly in relation to any change in the value of the "piece of paper". However, *Duru* was approved in *Kohn* and applied in *R. v. Mitchell* (1993) where the defendant was convicted of obtaining cheques from theatres by deception. In the latter, the court added that he had *mens rea* because he intended to deprive the theatres unless they paid to get them back (as cancelled cheques). Although not entirely satisfactory, this might be a better basis for arguing intent than the other reasons given in *Duru*.

---

**KEY PRINCIPLE:** *Under section 6(1), an intent is established in cases of borrowing or lending property if doing so "is for a period and in circumstances making it equivalent to an outright taking or disposal."*

## R. v. Lloyd, Bhuee & Ali 1985

The defendants took films, made master video tape copies, returned the films and sold pirate video tape versions. They were convicted of conspiracy to steal the films which rested on proof of intent to permanently deprive of the films.

**HELD:** (C.A.) Defendant's appeal allowed. Under section 6, borrowing only suffices if the intent is "to return the 'thing' in a such a changed state that it can truly be said that all its goodness or virtue has gone". This could not be said because the films still retained their virtue and value on return. [1985] 3 W.L.R. 30

**COMMENTARY**
Because the films had not lost all their virtue, the borrowing was not equivalent to an outright taking or disposal.

# Dishonesty

**KEY PRINCIPLE:** *A defendant is not dishonest if s/he believes s/he has a legal right to deprive the other of the property:* Theft Act 1968, *s.2(1)(a).*

**KEY PRINCIPLE:** *A defendant is not dishonest if s/he believes s/he would have consent from the person to whom the property belongs if that person knew of the circumstances of the appropriation:* Theft Act 1968, *s.2(1)(b).*

**KEY PRINCIPLE:** *A defendant is not dishonest if s/he believes that the person to whom the property belongs cannot be found by taking reasonable steps:* Theft Act 1968, *s.2(1)(c).*

**KEY PRINCIPLE:** *Where the defendant does not claim a belief falling under* Theft Act 1968, *s.2, the test for dishonesty is whether s/he realised that the conduct would be regarded as dishonest by ordinary people.*

## R. v. Ghosh 1982
A surgeon claimed fees that he was not entitled to. He was convicted of obtaining property by deception on a direction that dishonesty was to be tested by contemporary standards.

**HELD:** (C.A.) Defendant's appeal dismissed. Since dishonesty describes a state of mind, it must be established subjectively. The question is whether "according to the ordinary standards of reasonable and honest people what was done was dishonest . . . and if it was . . . whether the defendant himself must have realised that what he was doing was by those standards dishonest." On that test, the defendant was dishonest and so despite the misdirection there was no miscarriage of justice. [1982] Q.B. 1053

**COMMENTARY**
Although this case deals with *Theft Act 1968,* s.15 it also establishes the test of dishonesty for theft. The test is not purely subjective because a defendant is not judged by their own standard of honest behaviour but rather on their understanding of "ordinary" standards.

# 8. DECEPTION OFFENCES AND MAKING OFF WITHOUT PAYMENT

## Obtaining by deception

**KEY PRINCIPLE:** *There must be a false representation (of fact, law, or present intention).*

### R. v. Deller 1952

The defendant believed that the car he was selling was subject to a hire purchase agreement but said that it was "free from encumbrances". In fact this was probably true.

**HELD:** (C.A.) Defendant's appeal allowed. Although the defendant had *mens rea* (believing that his statement was false), the jury was entitled to conclude that the statement was not, in fact, false, so that the *actus reus* was missing. (1952) 36 Cr.App.R. 184

**COMMENTARY**
Attempting to obtain by deception covers this conduct.

**KEY PRINCIPLE:** *A deception may be expressed or implied from words or conduct.*

### R. v. Silverman 1988

A tradesman, who had built up a relationship of trust with the victims, overcharged them for work. He was convicted of obtaining money by the deception that the sum quoted was a "fair and proper" charge.

**HELD:** (C.A.) Defendant's appeal allowed due to an inadequate direction. The excessively high quotation could, in the circumstances, amount to a false representation: ". . . the appellant's silence on any matter other than the sums charged was . . . as eloquent as if he had said: '. . . we are going to get no more than a modest profit out of this' . . .". (1988) 86 Cr. App. R. 213

**COMMENTARY**
Since the defendant never expressly stated that the quotation was fair, the deception was implied. Whether or not an excessive quotation amounts to a deception depends on the circumstances. It probably did here because of the relationship of trust.

---

**KEY PRINCIPLE:** *An intention to pay before leaving can be implied from the conduct of ordering a meal in a restaurant.*

## D.P.P. v. Ray 1974

Intending to pay, the defendant ordered a meal in a restaurant. After eating, he decided not to pay, waited until the waiter left the room and then ran off. His appeal against conviction for evading liability by deception was allowed.

**HELD:** (H.L.) D.P.P.'s appeal allowed. A deception arose from the representation implied on ordering the meal: that he had the "means and intention of paying for it" before leaving. [1974] A.C. 370

**COMMENTARY**
This representation only applies if an order is "properly provided" which distinguishes *Guildford v. Lockyer* (1975) where no liability arose for leaving after the ordered meal did not arrive and an alternative was not acceptable. A similar representation can also be implied, for example, on entering a taxi or booking into a hotel: *R. v. Harris* (1975).

---

**KEY PRINCIPLE:** *The representation made on giving a cheque is that it will be met on presentment to the bank.*

## Metropolitan Police Commissioner v. Charles 1977

The defendant backed cheques with his cheque card thereby obliging his bank to meet the cheques although this created an unauthorised overdraft. The defendant appealed against conviction for obtaining a pecuniary advantage by deception.

**HELD:** (H.L.) Appeal dismissed for reasons given below. On giving a cheque, one represents that it will honoured on presentment. [1977] A.C. 177

## COMMENTARY
The representation is not that there are sufficient funds in the account to meet the cheque but simply that it will be met on the date specified. The same principle was applied to post-dated cheques in *R. v. Gilmartin* (1983).

---

**KEY PRINCIPLE:** *The representation made on using a cheque or credit card is that one has authority to use the card.*

## MPC v. Charles 1977
(see above).

**HELD:** (H.L.) Defendant's appeal dismissed. Whilst the implied representation that the cheque would be met was true (because it was backed by a guarantee card), a second representation was made on presenting the card. This was that the defendant had "actual authority from the bank to make a contract with the payee on the bank's behalf". This was a deception because the defendant was using the card in excess of his authority. [1977] A.C. 177

## COMMENTARY
For decisions based on similar principles see: *R. v. Lambie* (1982) (see p. 85) where presenting a Barclaycard implied authority to use it: *R. v. Sibartie* (1983) (see p. 91) where waving an underground season ticket at a station barrier implied authority to travel without further payment: *R. v. Hamilton* (1991) where presenting a signed cash withdrawal slip at the bank implied that the amount was owed to the defendant by the bank.

---

**KEY PRINCIPLE:** *A false representation may be implied from silence.*

## D.P.P. v. Ray 1974
(see p. 81).

**HELD:** (H.L.) The representation of intention to pay was true at the time of ordering but became false after the meal was eaten. The original representation had not ended but continued up to and including the point at which it became false. It continued for as long the defendant remained in the restaurant, "assuming the role of an ordinary customer". [1974] A.C. 370

**COMMENTARY**
This, in effect, gives rise to liability by omission. For another example of deception by silence/omission (where there was no continuing representation but there was a duty to disclose the truth)—*R. v. Firth* (1990) (see p. 90).

---

**KEY PRINCIPLE:** *"Obtaining" covers obtaining for oneself or for another.*

## R. v. Duru 1973

(see Chapter 7, p. 71). One ground for appeal was that the "mortgage" cheques from the G.L.C. were sent to solicitors acting for the mortgage applicants and were therefore never "obtained" by the defendants (who had committed the deception).

**HELD:** (C.A.) Appeal dismissed. There had been an obtaining of the cheques by the solicitors as a result of the defendant's deception and enabling another to obtain fell within *Theft Act 1968*, s.15(2). [1973] 3 All E.R. 715

**COMMENTARY**
All the obtaining offences can be committed by obtaining for another or enabling another to do so.

---

**KEY PRINCIPLE:** *There must be a causal link between the deception and the obtaining.*

## D.P.P. v. Ray 1974

(see p. 81).

**HELD:** (H.L.) Whether the deception causes the obtaining is a question of fact. Here it did because "the waiter was caused to refrain from taking certain courses of action which but for the representation he would have taken." [1974] A.C. 370

**COMMENTARY**

(1) It was probably only because the waiter left the room that the court could say that the deception operated on his mind, thereby causing the obtaining.

(2) Lord Morris referred to the diner who does not intend to pay from the outset who could also be charged with obtaining property (the meal) by deception. Presumably, it could also be obtaining a service (the cooking of the meal, etc.). However, in *Ray*, there could be no such charge because the deception arose after eating the meal. This is why the charge was one of evading liability because this was preceded (and caused) by the deception.

---

**KEY PRINCIPLE:** *Causation requires proof that the person "deceived" relied on the false representation alleged.*

## R. v. Laverty 1970

The defendant was convicted of obtaining property by the deception that a car sold was the original car bearing that number plate and chassis number. He appealed against conviction.

**HELD:** (C.A.) Appeal allowed. There was insufficient evidence that the statement alleged induced the purchase. The buyer's evidence was that he bought the car because he believed the defendant was its owner rather than because of the representation alleged. [1970] 3 All E.R. 432

**COMMENTARY**

(1) "Reliance" is normally established on the evidence of the person allegedly deceived. It requires proof that s/he would not have acted in the same way if the truth had been known. Here the evidence suggested that the buyer might have bought the car even if he had known the truth. Contrast *Charles* where causation was established by the casino manager is evidence that he only accepted the cheques because of the card and would not have done so if he had known that the defendant lacked authority.

(2) The importance of the evidence is also illustrated in *R. v. Talbott* (1995) (C.A.). The defendant received housing benefit after giving false details but was entitled to the benefit in any event. Nevertheless, causation was established because the

officers testified that they would not have paid her if they had known the truth.

## R. v. Lambie 1982

The defendant was charged with obtaining a pecuniary advantage by deception, having used her credit card to pay for goods in excess of her credit limit. The Court of Appeal allowed her appeal and the Crown appealed.

**HELD:** (H.L.) Appeal allowed. The shop manager gave evidence that it made no difference to her whether the defendant had sufficient credit. However, the representation in question was that the defendant had authority to use the card and it was permissible for the jury to infer that had the manager known that this authority was lacking she would not have completed the transaction. [1982] A.C. 449

**COMMENTARY**
One difficulty in these cases is that the issue of authority makes no difference to a seller who will receive payment anyway. However, the court inferred reliance because otherwise the inference was that the seller admitted participation in the other's fraud.

---

**KEY PRINCIPLE:** *The causal link is too remote if the representation is not an operative cause of the obtaining.*

## R. v. King & Stockwell 1987

The defendants deceived the victim into believing that her trees needed felling. They were convicted of attempting to obtain the felling fee by deception. They appealed on the basis that the operative cause of any payment would have been the work done not the deception.

**HELD:** (C.A.) Appeal dismissed. Operative cause was a question of fact, applying the test of "direct connection between the pretence" and the obtaining. On the facts, there was sufficient evidence that the money would have been paid as a result of the lies told. [1987] 1 Q.B. 547

**COMMENTARY**
(1) The defence relied on *R. v. Lewis* (1922) (Assize Ct.) where a teacher was appointed after lying about her qualifications. She was not guilty of obtaining property (her salary) by

deception because it was held that this was obtained by the work done and not by the deception. The causal link was too remote (although she might, today, be guilty of obtaining the more closely connected pecuniary advantage, the job opportunity). *Lewis* was distinguished because in *King* the deception was more directly linked to receipt of the money. For other cases to compare on causation, see *R. v. Clucas* (1949) and *R. v. Button* (1900).

(2) Whilst the deception must not be too remote and must be an operative cause, it need not be the sole cause. This is further illustrated in *R. v. Miller* (1993) where the Court of Appeal approved *King*, holding that the jury was entitled to conclude that a false representation that a vehicle was a taxi was one (although not the sole) cause of the fare being obtained. This might also assist in explaining the decision in *Talbott*.

# Theft Act 1968, s.15—Obtaining Property

**KEY PRINCIPLE:** *The definition of "property", "belonging to another" and "intention permanently to deprive" are the same as for theft.*

## R. v. Duru 1973
(see Chapter 7, p. 71).

**COMMENTARY**
This case dealt with s15 and illustrates that property includes "things in action" (the cheques belonging to the G.L.C.). It also illustrates the meaning of intention to permanently deprive. [1973] 3 All E.R. 715

# Theft Act 1968, s.16—Obtaining a Pecuniary Advantage

**KEY PRINCIPLE:** *Obtaining a pecuniary advantage includes being "allowed to borrow by way of overdraft . . ." section 16(2)(b).*

## Metropolitan Police Commissioner v. Charles 1977
(see p. 81).

**COMMENTARY**
(1) The defendant committed s16(2)(b) by creating the unauthorised overdraft. "Allowed to borrow" therefore covers "forcing" a bank to create an overdraft by using a cheque guarantee card. This offence should have been charged in *Navvabi* (see Chapter 7, p. 71).
(2) s.16(2)(b) also covers taking out insurance policies and annuity contracts or obtaining an improvement of the terms on which allowed to do so.

---

**KEY PRINCIPLE:** *Obtaining a pecuniary advantage includes being 'given the opportunity to earn remuneration or greater remuneration in an office or employment . . ." s.16(2)(c).*

## R. v. Callender 1993

The defendant was convicted under section 16(2)(c), having falsely represented that he had particular accountancy qualifications and membership. He appealed on the basis that a self-employed accountant did not fall within the terms "office or employment" because there was no relationship of master and servant between himself and clients.

**HELD:** (C.A.) Appeal dismissed. "Office or employment" were not restricted to contracts of service but bore their ordinary meaning which covered "employment" as an independent contractor. [1993] Q.B. 303

**COMMENTARY**
(1) A charge under this section would avoid the problems encountered in *Lewis* since the offence is committed on gaining "the opportunity to earn . . ."
(2) section 16(2)(b) also covers being given the opportunity "to win money by betting".

# Theft Act 1978, s.1—Obtaining Services

**KEY PRINCIPLE:** *A service is a non-gratuitous benefit conferred by the doing of an act, or by causing or permitting an act to be done.*

## R. v. Halai 1983

The defendant was convicted of obtaining (and attempting to obtain) services, having used false details to obtain; a surveyor's report and valuation; the opening of a building society's savings account; and an attempt to obtain a mortgage advance.

**HELD:** (C.A.) The opening of the account was not a service because no benefit was conferred and no payment was made or expected for doing so. The mortgage advance was also not a service. The survey was a service, being both of benefit to the defendant and something for which payment was expected. [1983] Crim.L.R. 624

### COMMENTARY
In *R. v. Shortland* (1995), (C.A.), opening bank accounts under false names did not fall within s.1 because there was no evidence adduced that this was to be paid for. The implication is that had such evidence been presented, it would have been a service. A mortgage advance should also be a service being both a benefit and non-gratuitous. The Law Commission recommended that *Halai* be reversed on this point and in *R. v. Widdowson* (1986), the Court of Appeal held, distinguishing *Halai*, that a hire purchase agreement was a service.

## Theft Act 1978, s.2—Obtaining Evasion of Liability

**KEY PRINCIPLE:** *"Securing remission" under section 2(1)(a) may require proof that the creditor believes an existing debt is being extinguished.*

### R. v. Jackson 1983
The defendant "paid" for petrol with a stolen Access card. He was convicted under *Theft Act 1978*, s.2(1)(a) and appealed.

**HELD:** (C.A.) Appeal dismissed. He had secured remission because the trader, having accepted the card, would look to Access and not the defendant for payment. [1983] Crim.L.R. 617

### COMMENTARY
(1) The fact that the creditor thought that the card extinguished liability was sufficient to give rise to section 2(1)(a). The argument that the debt *actually* has to be extinguished was doubted in *R. v. Holt & Lee* (1981) (see below).

(2) There could be no charge for obtaining property (the petrol) by deception because the use of the card (the deception) occurred after property had passed.

---

**KEY PRINCIPLE:** *"Inducing a creditor to forgo payment" of an existing liability under section 2(1)(b) may be committed by persuading the creditor that no liability is owed.*

## R. v. Holt & Lee 1981

The defendants were convicted of attempting section 2(1)(b) by falsely representing that they had already paid the bill for a meal.

**HELD:** (C.A.) Defendant's appeal dismissed. The three subsections create three separate offences. All of the elements necessary to establish an attempted section 2(1)(b) were present on the facts and so the defendants were rightly convicted. [1981] 1 W.L.R. 1000

### COMMENTARY

It is suggested that the defendants were not guilty of section 2(1)(a) because there was no intent on the part of the creditor to remit the liability (having been deceived into believing that it did not exist).

---

**KEY PRINCIPLE:** *Inducing a creditor to take a cheque in payment amounts to inducing the creditor to "wait for payment" (s.2(1)(b))*

## R. v. Hammond 1982

The defendant "paid" for repairs done on his car by a cheque that he knew would "bounce". He was charged under s.2(1)(b) and *Theft Act 1978*, s.3.

**HELD:** (Cr. Ct.): On the facts, the charge under s.2(1)(b) was appropriate. [1982] Crim.L.R. 611

### COMMENTARY

Section 2(3) provides that "for the purposes of subsection (1)(b) a person induced to take . . . a cheque . . . is to be treated not as being paid but as being induced to wait for payment."

Contrast the position regarding "dud" cheques under *Theft Act 1968*, s.3.

---

**KEY PRINCIPLE:** *"Inducing the creditor to forgo or wait for payment" of an existing liability under s.2(1)(b) requires proof of intention to make permanent default.*

## R. v. Holt & Lee 1981

(see p. 89).

**HELD:** (C.A.) The court noted that s.2(1)(b) required proof of intent to make permanent default which was not the case in subsections (a) and (c). [1981] 1 W.L.R. 1000

---

**KEY PRINCIPLE:** *"Obtaining exemption or abatement" under section 2(1)(c) does not require proof of an existing liability and can be committed by omission.*

## R. v. Firth 1990

The defendant was convicted under s.2(1)(c), having failed to inform hospitals that his patients were private, thereby avoiding treatment charges. He appealed on the basis that deception could not be committed by omission and that, if it could, there was no liability to pay in existence at the time of the deception.

**HELD:** (C.A.) Appeal dismissed. Since the defendant had a duty to give the information to the hospital, refraining from doing so could give rise to liability under section 2(1)(c). Moreover, since section 2(1)(a) and (b) specify an "existing liability", the fact that Parliament omitted the term from subsection (c) could be regarded as deliberate. Therefore there is no need for an existing liability under s.2(1)(c). (1990) 91 Cr.App.R. 217

### COMMENTARY
The defendant used deception to prevent the liability from arising rather than using a deception to avoid an existing liability. Thus he could not have been guilty of either subsection (a) or (b) but could be guilty of (c).

---

**KEY PRINCIPLE:** *The three subsections overlap and are not mutually exclusive.*

## R. v. Sibartie 1983

The defendant was convicted of attempting to commit section 2(1)(c) of the *Theft Act 1978* having deceived ticket collectors into believing that he had paid for the whole of his underground journey.

**HELD:** (C.A.) Defendant's appeal dismissed. There was an overlap between the three subsections and the fact that this conduct might amount to attempting section 2(1)(b) did not prevent it from also falling under section 2(1)(c). [1983] Crim. L.R. 470

### COMMENTARY
The existence of a liability to pay did not prevent section 2(1)(c) from arising because (c) covers both existing and prospective liabilities. Whilst the conduct also amounted to section 2(1)(b), it presumably did not amount to section 2(1)(a) because the ticket collector did not intend to remit liability (having been deceived into believing that there was none).

## R. v. Jackson 1983
(see p. 88).

**Held:** (C.A.) *Holt & Lee* had not decided that the three sub-paragraphs were mutually exclusive and so whilst the conduct in this case amounted to section 2(1)(a), the fact that it might also have amounted to section 2(1)(b) was irrelevant.

# *Mens Rea* of Deception Offences

**KEY PRINCIPLE:** *The deception must be deliberate or reckless and the obtaining must be dishonest.*

## R. v. Ghosh 1982
(See Chapter 7, p. 79).

### COMMENTARY
*Ghosh* establishes the sole definition of dishonesty in deception offences. Both elements of the *mens rea* must be proved separately. Even where a deception is deliberate (despite comments to the contrary in *Ghosh*) it does not follow that the obtaining was dishonest. An illustration is *Talbott* where although the defendant deliberately lied to local authority

officers, she could, presumably, have pleaded that she was not dishonest because she believed that she was, in law, entitled to the housing benefit.

# Making Off Without Payment

**KEY PRINCIPLE:** *The defendant must make off (depart) from the spot where payment is expected or required for goods supplied or services done.*

## R. v. Aziz 1993

The defendant refused to pay a taxi fare on arrival at his destination and so the driver was driving to a police station when the defendant ran off. He was convicted under s3 and appealed on the basis that the spot where payment was expected or required was his destination and not from where he had made off.

**HELD:** (C.A.) Appeal dismissed. "Makes off" involves departing without paying from the place where payment is usually made, which varies from case to case. There was a making off on these facts. [1993] Crim.L.R. 708

**COMMENTARY**
In this case the making off was without payment for services done (the taxi ride) and the offence covers any legally enforceable provision of services (such as the provision of hotel accommodation, *R. v. Allen* (1985) (see p. 93) and repairs done on a car, *R. v. Hammond* (1982) (see p. 89). It also covers the supply of goods, such as a meal in a restaurant, in which case, the "spot" varies according to the nature of the restaurant (it might, for example, be at the table or at the exit point).

---

**KEY PRINCIPLE:** *The expectation (or requirement) of payment must be legally enforceable.*

## Troughton v. Metropolitan Police Commissioner 1987

A taxi driver was unable to get destination details from a drunken passenger and so drove to the nearest police station. The defendant was convicted of making off without payment of the fare and appealed.

**HELD:** (D.C.) Appeal allowed. The driver had breached the contract by not completing the journey. Therefore he was not legally entitled to require payment of the fare and so the defendant was not guilty. [1987] Crim.L.R. 138

---

KEY PRINCIPLE: *The defendant must make off without having paid. There is no such making off if a cheque is accepted in "payment".*

## R. v. Hammond 1982

(see p. 89).

**HELD:** (Cr. Ct.) The defendant did not make off without payment because the garage accepted the cheque without a cheque guarantee card and allowed the defendant to leave. [1982] Crim.L.R. 611

### COMMENTARY
This is a difficult case. Does it decide that the "consent" of the garage prevented a making off or is it that the cheque was "payment"? The judge distinguished the case of counterfeit money on the basis that the recipient does not know that s/he is taking a risk as s/he does with an unbacked cheque. This suggests that it is not the "allowing the defendant to leave" that prevents a making off, because that applies equally to counterfeit money. The difference is that counterfeit money is not legal tender but a cheque is. Therefore, it might be that a cheque (even a "dud" one) is treated as payment for the purposes of section 3 but not for section 2(1)(b). However, it is hard to see how a "dud" cheque is payment as "required or expected".

---

KEY PRINCIPLE: *The defendant must intend to make permanent default.*

## R. v. Allen 1985

The defendant left a hotel without paying his bill but claimed to intend to pay in due course. The Court of Appeal allowed his appeal against conviction and the Crown appealed.

**HELD:** (H.L.) Appeal dismissed. The reference in section 3 to "intent to avoid payment" means "intention to evade payment altogether" [1985] 1 A.C. 1029

**COMMENTARY**

The other elements to the *mens rea* of section 3 are knowledge that payment is expected or required and dishonesty (as defined in *Ghosh*).

---

# 9. OTHER OFFENCES CONTRARY TO THE THEFT ACTS

## Robbery

**KEY PRINCIPLE:** *The defendant must use force on a person or seek to put a person in fear of force immediately before or at the time of stealing.*

### R. v. Hale 1978

The defendant put his hand over a woman's mouth to prevent screaming whilst the other searched her house. The latter returned with jewellery and the defendants tied and gagged the woman to make their escape. The defendant was convicted and appealed against the direction that using force to effect an escape was sufficient for robbery.

**HELD:** (C.A.) Appeal dismissed. It was for the jury to decide, as matter of common sense, when the act of appropriation finished. Therefore it was open for them to decide that robbery occurred when the force was used immediately before or at the time of the theft, which still continued to the time that the victim was bound and gagged. (1978) 68 Cr. App. R. 415

**COMMENTARY**

(1) The *actus reus* and *mens rea* of theft must be established. In this case, appropriation was a continuing act (compare *R.v. Pitham & Hehl* (1976) (see p. 69) and *Atakpu* (see Chapter 7, p. 68)). *R v. Lockley* (1995) decided that *Gomez* (see Chapter 7, p. 67) had not affected *Hale* and appropriation could still be continuous so that the defendants were guilty of robbery when they used force after taking beer from an off-licence.

(2) The force must be used on a person and not just against property but the person need not be the one to whom the property belongs.

**KEY PRINCIPLE:** *The meaning of "force" is to be left to the jury.*

## R. v. Dawson & James 1976

The victim's wallet was stolen by one of three men whilst he was being jostled by the others. The defendant appealed against conviction for robbery on the basis that this was insufficient evidence of "force".

**HELD:** (C.A.) Appeal dismissed. "Force" has an ordinary meaning and was for a jury to decide. (1978) 68 Cr.App.R. 170

---

**KEY PRINCIPLE:** *The force or "threat" must be used in order to steal.*

## R. v. Donaghy 1981

The defendants threatened a minicab driver into taking them from Newmarket to London. Once they arrived, they stole his money.

**HELD:** (Cr. Ct) The jury acquitted, following a direction that the threats must continue until the time of the theft and be used to obtain the money. [1981] Crim. L.R. 644

**COMMENTARY**

The jury may have decided either that the threat was too remote from the theft or that it was used to get the ride to London rather than "in order to steal".

# Burglary

**KEY PRINCIPLE:** *The defendant must make effective and substantial entry into a building or part of a building.*

## R. v. Collins 1973

The defendant appealed against conviction for burglary with intent to rape. He had entered the bedroom of a young woman who he believed to be inviting him in. There was evidence that he had intended to rape her if she did not consent but they had consensual sexual intercourse until she realised that he was not her boyfriend, as she had thought. A crucial issue was whether the defendant had entered the bedroom via the window before or after the woman appeared to be inviting him in.

**HELD:** (C.A.) Appeal allowed for reasons discussed below. Edmund-Davies L.J. commented that the first element of burglary was that the defendant entered the building in an "effective and substantial" manner. [1973] 1 Q.B. 100

**COMMENTARY**
*Theft Act 1968*, s.9 creates two offences: entry as a trespasser with ulterior intent (section 9(1)(a)) and entry as a trespasser and commission of an ulterior offence (section 9(1)(b)). Both require proof of substantial and effective entry.

## R. v. Walkington 1979

The defendant was convicted of burglary with intent to steal, having been arrested in a department store, searching through a till, inside a three-sided counter. He appealed on the basis that he had not entered the store as a trespasser.

**HELD:** (C.A.) Appeal dismissed. The elements of section 9 included entry to part of a building. The physical partition of the counter was sufficient to mark it off as part of a building into which the defendant had entered. [1979] 2 All E.R. 716

---

**KEY PRINCIPLE:** *The entry must be "as a trespasser".*

## R. v. Walkington 1979
(see above)

**COMMENTARY**
The case illustrates that whilst entry to the building may not be "as a trespasser", entry into a part of the building (the three-sided counter) for which one has no permission will suffice.

## R. v. Jones & Smith 1976

The defendants entered Smith's father's house with intent to steal two televisions. They were convicted of burglary under section 9(1)(b) (on the basis of entering the house as trespassers and stealing therein). They claimed that Smith was not a trespasser because he had his father's permission to enter the house.

**HELD:** (C.A.) Appeal dismissed. Whilst a person with general permission to enter premises would not normally be a trespasser, entry with the sole intention of stealing once inside was entry in excess of permission and so trespass. [1976] 3 All E.R. 54

## COMMENTARY
Both s.9 offences require that the defendant enter as a trespasser. The doctrine of trespass ab initio does not apply to burglary: *Collins*. Therefore exceeding one's licence after entry does not in itself make the entry a trespass. It was the criminal intention of the defendants on entry in *Jones* that destroyed the permission. This may be contrasted with *Collins* (discussed below). Note also that the implication from *Collins* is that permission to enter may come from the occupier or from the victim of the intended or ulterior offence.

---

**KEY PRINCIPLE:** *The defendant must know that s/he is trespassing or be reckless as to the trespass.*

## R. v. Collins 1973
(see p. 95)

**HELD:** (C.A.) Appeal allowed due to a misdirection on the *mens rea*. The defendant must know that he is trespassing or be reckless as to the fact. If the defendant had already 'entered' the window before believing that he was being invited in, he was guilty of burglary. If he had not yet entered, he was entitled to the defence that he had not trespassed because he believed that he had consent for entry. [1973] 1 Q.B. 100

## COMMENTARY
(1) Note that the *mens rea* must exist at the time of entry if section 9(1)(a) is charged whilst *mens rea* at any point during the commission of the ulterior offence satisfies section 9(1)(b).
(2) *Collins* was referred to in *Jones & Smith* where the court concluded that the boys were trespassers because they knew that they were entering in excess of the permission given. Whilst *Collins* deals with the *mens rea* of the offence, there is a problem in explaining why, like *Jones*, his criminal intent (to rape) did not destroy any permission to enter (in which case it could similarly be said that he knew he was entering in excess of permission). However, whilst the defendants in *Jones* knew that they were not given permission to enter to steal televisions, Collins may have believed that he was given

permission to enter for sex (although he clearly was not given permission to enter to rape). There are other differences between the cases. The permission in *Collins* was specific—to enter for sex, whilst in *Jones* it was general—to use the house whenever. Moreover, the criminal intention in *Jones* is described as unconditional whilst that in *Collins* was conditional.

---

**KEY PRINCIPLE:** *Under Theft Act 1968, s.9(1)(a) the entry must be with intent to steal, inflict grievous bodily harm, rape, or do unlawful damage*

**COMMENTARY**
The defendant must intend to commit the offence in question in the building entered as a trespasser. *Collins* and *Walkington* are examples of charges under this section.

---

**KEY PRINCIPLE:** *Theft Act 1968, Under s.9(1)(b), the defendant must commit the ulterior offence of theft, attempted theft, inflicting or attempting to inflict grievous bodily harm.*

**COMMENTARY**
*Jones & Smith* is an example of a charge under this section.

# Aggravated Burglary

**KEY PRINCIPLE:** *The defendant must have a firearm, explosive or weapon of offence at the time of the burglary* (Theft Act 1968, s.10.)

## R. v. Francis 1982

The defendants were armed with sticks, either just before or on entry to a building, which they then discarded. At the time of entry there was no criminal intent but after entry the defendants stole from the house. They were convicted of aggravated burglary on a direction that it was sufficient that they were armed on entry to the house.

**HELD:** (C.A.) Defendant's appeal allowed. The aggravating article must be present at the time of the burglary. The relevant time under section 9(1)(a), which did not apply on the facts, was at the point of entry. The relevant time under section 9(1)(b), which did apply, was at the time of the ulterior offence by which time the sticks had been discarded. [1982] Crim. L.R. 363

## COMMENTARY
The meaning of firearm, explosive and weapon of offence are explained further in *Theft Act 1968*, s.10.

# Blackmail

**KEY PRINCIPLE:** *The defendant must make a demand.*

## R. v. Collister & Warhurst 1955

Two police officers were charged with demanding money with menaces. One told the other, in the hearing of the victim, that the victim had been importuning him but implied that a report might not be filed. At a following meeting the victim was asked whether he had brought anything with him at which point he handed over money to the defendants.

**HELD:** (C.C.A.) The trial judge had been correct to direct that there need not be an express demand. Demeanour and circumstances might make it possible to imply that a demand was being made (and being backed by threats). (1955) 39 Cr. App. R 100

## COMMENTARY
The offence is complete on making the demand (with menaces). It is not necessary that an oral demand actually be heard or a written one received: *Treacy v. D.P.P.* (1971).

---

**KEY PRINCIPLE:** *The demand must be accompanied by menaces.*

## R. v. Garwood 1987

The defendant was convicted of blackmail having made a demand of someone who was timid and more likely to feel menaced than an ordinary person. The judge directed that the victim's timidity did not prevent the finding of a menace.

**HELD:** (C.A.) Defendant's appeal dismissed. There had been a misdirection but no miscarriage of justice. Threats that might affect the ordinary stable person but which do not affect the victim can still be menaces. Where a threat affects the victim but might not affect a person of normal stability it must be shown that the defendant knew of the likely effect on the victim before it can be said to be a menace. [1987] 1 All E.R. 1032

---

**KEY PRINCIPLE:** *The demand must be unwarranted. It will be warranted if the defendant believes that there are reasonable grounds for making the demand and that menaces are a proper means for enforcing the demand.*

## R. v. Harvey & Others 1980

The defendants were "swindled" in a cannabis deal by the victim. They kidnapped his wife and child and threatened them and the victim if their money was not returned. They were convicted of blackmail and appealed against a direction that the demand could not be warranted because the menaces involved threats to commit criminal acts.

**HELD:** (C.A.) Appeal dismissed although the direction was not strictly correct. The test was subjective and so the question was whether the defendants believed the menace to be a "proper" (lawful, not criminal) means for enforcing the demand. (1980) 72 Cr. App. R. 139

**COMMENTARY**
In this case, the defendants probably believed that they had reasonable grounds for making the demand but they failed to satisfy the latter part of the test.

---

**KEY PRINCIPLE:** *The demand must be made with a view to gain or intent to cause loss.*

## R. v. Bevans 1988

The defendant, who suffered a painful medical condition, called a doctor. When he arrived, the defendant, armed with a gun, threatened to shoot him unless he gave a pain killing injection. The defendant was convicted of blackmail and appealed on the basis that his actions had not been with intent to gain or cause loss.

**HELD:** (C.A.) Appeal dismissed. *Theft Act, 1968*, s.34(2) specifies that the "gain" or "loss" must be in money or other property. The pain killing liquid was property that the defendant was aiming to gain and so the offence was established. (1988) 87 Cr.App.R. 64

# Handling Stolen Goods

**KEY PRINCIPLE:** *The goods must be stolen goods when handled.*

## Re Attorney-General's Reference (No. 1 of 1974)

Suspecting that goods in a car had been stolen, a police officer immobilised the car and waited for its driver who was then charged with handling stolen goods. The trial judge directed an acquittal on the basis that the goods had been restored to the lawful possession or custody of the police officer and had therefore ceased to be stolen under Theft Act 1968 s.24(3).

**HELD:** (C.A.) Whether or not the goods ceased to be stolen depended on the state of mind of the police officer. If by immobilising the car, he intended to reduce the goods into his possession or control ("take charge of them so that they could not be removed"), they had ceased to be stolen. However, if he simply intended to prevent the driver from driving away before answering questions, he may not have reduced the goods into his possession or control and so they were still stolen. The trial judge had therefore incorrectly withdrawn the question of the purpose of the officer from the jury. [1974] 2 All E.R. 899

**COMMENTARY**
(1) Other cases on this point include *R. v. King* (1938) and *Haughton v. Smith* (1975). Goods also cease to be stolen if restored to the person from whom they were stolen.
(2) "Goods" has much the same meaning as for theft and "stolen" means having been the subject of theft, blackmail or *Theft Act 1968*, s.15. They also include goods directly or indirectly representing stolen goods (see *Theft Act 1968*, s.24(2)).

---

**KEY PRINCIPLE:** *The goods must be handled "otherwise than in the course of stealing" (i.e. after they have been stolen).*

## R. v. Pitham & Hehl 1976
(see Chapter 7, p. 69).

**HELD:** (C.A.) Defendant's appeal dismissed. Since the appropriation (and theft) was complete on offering the furniture for sale, the actions of the defendants thereafter were not 'in the course of stealing' and so could be handling. (1976) 65 Cr. App. R. 45

### COMMENTARY
Much turns on the duration of appropriation (as in robbery). Here the court rejected the argument that appropriation continued until the furniture was loaded into the van, deciding instead that it was an "instantaneous" act. For other decisions on the issue in a different context see *Atakpu* (Chapter 7, p. 68) and *Hale* (p. 94).

---

**KEY PRINCIPLE:** *There are two offences of handling. The first consists of receiving or arranging to receive stolen goods.*

## R. v. Bloxham 1983
The defendant bought a car which he did not know had been stolen. Discovering that it had, he sold it and was convicted of handling by undertaking or assisting in the disposal or realisation of the car for the benefit of the purchaser. He appealed on the basis that his acts had not been undertaken for the benefit of another.

**HELD:** (H.L.) Appeal allowed for reasons given below. Lord Bridge explained that *Theft Act 1968*, s.22 creates "two distinct offences" of handling. The first being receiving or arranging to receive. [1983] 1 A.C. 109

### COMMENTARY
The first handling offence could not be charged because the defendant lacked *mens rea* when he received (bought) the car.

---

**KEY PRINCIPLE:** *Receiving occurs when the defendant comes into possession or control of the goods.*

## R. v. Brook 1993

The defendant's wife found a bag containing stolen cheques and cards. She told the defendant what was in the bag and he suggested that they put it in his car whilst deciding what to do. He was convicted of handling by receiving and the issue on appeal related to the *mens rea* of the offence.

**HELD:** (C.A.) Appeal allowed for reasons given below. Receipt was complete on coming into possession (control) of the goods. This was when, knowing what was in the bag, the defendant told his wife to put it into the car. [1993] Crim.L.R. 455

---

**KEY PRINCIPLE:** *The second form of handling is by undertaking or assisting in the retention, removal, disposal or realisation of goods or arranging to do so. This must be done for the benefit of another.*

## R. v. Bloxham 1983

(see p. 102).

**HELD:** (H.L.) Defendant's appeal allowed. The second handling offence covers four activities committed in one of two ways: the defendant undertakes the activity for another's benefit or another undertakes the activity and is assisted by the defendant. The "other" is limited in the same way in both parts. A purchaser of stolen goods cannot be "another person" (for whose benefit an activity is undertaken) because the act of purchase does not fall into one of the four activities (retention, removal, disposal or realisation). Therefore, although a sale might be a disposal or realisation for the purchaser's benefit, it does not fall within the section. [1983] A.C. 109

**COMMENTARY**
The four activities are different: retention means "keep possession of . . . continue to have": *R. v. Pitchley* (1972) (below); removal means transporting or carrying; disposal covers getting rid of or transforming; and realisation is selling.

---

**KEY PRINCIPLE:** *"Assisting in" retention, removal, disposal or realisation requires something done that helps or encourages for the purpose of enabling the specified activity.*

## R. v. Kanwar 1982

The defendant lied to the police about stolen goods in her home in order to protect her husband who had stolen them.

**HELD:** (C.A.) Merely using stolen goods (or keeping them in the house) was not sufficient to amount to assisting in their retention. Concealing goods was sufficient and lying to the police amounted to assisting in retention for the benefit of her husband. [1982] 2 All E.R. 528

**COMMENTARY**

See also *R. v. Pitchley* (1972) where, having received stolen money from his son without knowing it was stolen, the defendant paid it into a post office savings account. Having discovered that it was stolen, he left the money in the account which amounted to assisting in its retention for his son's benefit. This case, unlike *Kanwar*, appears to impose liability for assisting by omission.

## R. v. Coleman 1986

The defendant knew his wife had stolen money from her employers and this was used to cover their expenses and to purchase a flat. He was convicted of assisting in the disposal of the money.

**HELD:** (C.A.) Defendant's appeal allowed. Simply getting the benefit from the disposal did not amount to assisting in it which required proof of some act of encouragement, agreement or help. [1986] Crim. L.R. 56

**KEY PRINCIPLE:** *The* mens rea *(knowledge or belief that the goods are stolen and dishonesty) must exist at the time of the act alleged to be the handling.*

## R. v. Brook 1993

(see p. 103).

**HELD:** (C.A.) Defendant's appeal allowed due to a misdirection relating to the timing of the mens rea. If charged with receiving, the *mens rea* must exist at the point of coming into possession (and not any time thereafter). Moreover, the test for belief that goods are stolen is subjective not objective. [1993] Crim.L.R. 455

**COMMENTARY**

Contrast handling by undertaking or assisting in the four activities where *mens rea* formed at any point during the continuance of doing so is sufficient. Knowledge or belief that the goods are stolen (and not mere suspicion) is required but this is satisfied where a defendant "shuts his eyes to the obvious": *Pitchley*. The doctrine of recent possession and *Theft Act 1968*, s.27(3) can assist in proof of *mens rea*.

# 10. CRIMINAL DAMAGE AND ARSON

## Criminal Damage Act 1971, s.1(1)

**KEY PRINCIPLE:** *Property belonging to another must be damaged or destroyed. 'Damage' includes temporary impairment of property.*

### Hardman v. C.C. of Avon & Somerset 1986

Members of C.N.D. were convicted of criminal damage having painted figures on a pavement in soluble whitewash. They appealed on the basis that there was no damage because the paint would wash away.

**HELD:** (Cr. Ct.): Appeal dismissed. Damage covered "mischief done to property" and, having caused expense and inconvenience to the Local Authority in removing the graffiti, damage had been done. [1986] Crim.L.R. 330

**COMMENTARY**

(1) "Damage" covers not only permanent or temporary physical damage but also impairment of usefulness or value. See *R. v. Whiteley* (1991) (below). Where the damage or destruction is caused by fire, it is arson by virtue of s.1(3).

(2) The property must belong to another: anyone with custody, control, a proprietary right or interest or charge on it: section 10(2).

**KEY PRINCIPLE:** *The property damaged or destroyed must be tangible but the damage need not be tangible.*

## R. v. Whiteley 1991

A hacker gained access to an academic network and, *inter alia*, deleted and added files, left messages and changed passwords. He was convicted of damaging the computer discs and appealed on the basis that destruction or alteration of information on discs was damage to intangible property (not covered by the Act).

**HELD:** (C.A.) Appeal dismissed. The damage done was intangible but the Act does not require tangible damage. The property damaged must be tangible which it was because he impaired the usefulness and value of the discs which were tangible property. The court also referred to the *Computer Misuse Act 1990* which now creates an offence of (and excludes from criminal damage) unauthorised modification of computer material. (1991) 93 Cr.App.R. 25

### COMMENTARY

Section 10(1) defines property in much the same way as for theft except that land can be the subject of criminal damage without exception and intangible property cannot. This case decides (as did *Cox v. Riley* (1986) where a computer program was erased from a circuit card) that damage to intangible property (*e.g.* data or computer programs) does not fall within the Act but is included if by so doing the defendant damages tangible property (*e.g.* discs or circuit cards).

---

**KEY PRINCIPLE:** *The mens rea of criminal damage is satisfied by proof of Caldwell-style recklessness.*

## R. v. Caldwell 1982

(see Chapter 2, p. 18).

**HELD:** (H.L.) A defendant is reckless when, having created an obvious risk of damage to property belonging to another, s/he either gives no thought to the risk or recognises some risk and carries on regardless. [1982] A.C. 341

### COMMENTARY

The test for inadvertent recklessness is whether the risk would be obvious to the reasonable person: *Elliott v. C.* (1983) (see Chapter 2, p. 19). The purely objective nature of the test was confirmed in two cases under *Criminal*

*Damage Act 1971*, s.1(2): *Stephen (Malcolm R.)* (1984) (see Chapter 2, p. 20) and *R. v. Sangha* (1988) (see p. 109). It was also applied in *R. v. Cole* (1994) (C.A.) so that a 15-year old boy of low mental capacity was guilty under section 1(2) because the risk of endangerment involved in his setting fire to a haystack when friends were sleeping nearby would have been obvious to a reasonable person. Criminal damage can also be committed intentionally.

---

**KEY PRINCIPLE:** *A defendant who concludes that there is no risk of damage does not commit criminal damage.*

## C.C. of Avon v. Shimmen 1987
(see Chapter 2, p. 20).

**COMMENTARY**
The case confirms that realising a risk of damage but thinking that it has been minimised amounts to recklessness but mistakenly thinking that there is no risk at all does not.

---

**KEY PRINCIPLE:** *Belief that the person entitled to consent to the damage or destruction had consented or would have done so if they had known of the circumstances amounts to lawful excuse:* Criminal Damage Act 1971, *s.5(2)(a).*

## R. v. Denton 1982
The defendant set fire to machinery, having been asked by his employer to do so. He appealed against conviction for criminal damage.

**HELD:** (C.A.) Appeal allowed. Honest belief that his employer (the person entitled to consent) had consented amounted to a lawful excuse under *Criminal Damage Act 1971*, s.5(2)(a). Moreover, since the owner consented, there was lawful excuse under section 1(1) even without recourse to section 5(2)(a). [1982] 1 All E.R. 65

**COMMENTARY**
The belief has to be honest but does not have to be based on reasonable grounds. Thus a defendant may rely on this belief where it is caused by self-induced intoxication: *Jaggard v. Dickinson* (1981), (see Chapter 13, p. 139). Nevertheless, a belief, however genuine, that God consented to (or instructed

one to do) the damage does not amount to lawful excuse: see Blake v. D.P.P. (1993) (D.C.) where a vicar unsuccessfully tried, *inter alia*, to use this defence, having written a Biblical quote on a pillar in protest about the use of military force in the Gulf.

---

**KEY PRINCIPLE:** *A defendant has lawful excuse under section 5(2)(b), if the damage was done to protect other property that the defendant believed to be in immediate need of protection and in the belief that the means adopted were reasonable in the circumstances.*

### R. v. Hill & Hall 1989

Members of CND were convicted under *Criminal Damage Act 1971*, s.3 for being in possession of a hacksaw blade, intending to use it to cut through the perimeter fence of a U.S. base. They claimed the lawful excuse that they were aiming to protect property in the U.K. from the risk of a nuclear strike by "persuading" the U.S. to withdraw their base.

**HELD:** (C.A.) Application for leave to appeal refused. The defendant's belief was subjectively judged, but, on the facts as the defendant believed them to be, the action must be objectively capable of protecting property. It was not so here because the actions taken were too remote from that eventual aim. Moreover, the section requires that the defendant believes that the property is in immediate need of protection and there was no evidence that the defendants believed that the nuclear threat was immediate. (1989) 89 Cr.App.R. 74

**COMMENTARY**
The same conclusion was reached in *Blake v. D.P.P.* (1993) where the vicar also unsuccessfully pleaded that his actions were done to protect property in the Gulf States because the causal link was too remote. A similar conclusion on immediacy was also reached in rejecting his defence of duress of circumstances (see Chapter 14).

## Criminal Damage Act 1971, s.1(2)

**KEY PRINCIPLE:** *The "aggravated" offence under s.1(2) does not require proof of actual endangerment but requires* *proof of intent to endanger life or recklessness in relation to endangering life.*

## R. v. Sangha 1988

The defendants caused a fire in a flat which was temporarily unoccupied. Moreover, because of the way the buildings were constructed there was no danger of the fire spreading to other flats. The defendants were convicted of criminal damage (arson) contrary to section 1(2) on the basis of recklessness as to whether life would be endangered. They appealed on the ground that (albeit unknown to them) there was no obvious risk of endangerment due to factors that prevented a risk from materialising.

**HELD:** (C.A.) Appeal dismissed. Section 1(2) did not require that an actual danger to life existed. It was sufficient that the defendants intended such a danger or were reckless about it. For reasons given below, the defendants had been reckless and so the offence was established. [1988] 2 All E.R. 385

### COMMENTARY

Because this was a case of criminal damage contrary to section 1(2), committed by fire, it is charged as arson: section 1(3). The point was also made in *Steer* (1987) (see below) that the offence under section 1(2) is simply an aggravated form of section 1(1), satisfied by the same *actus reus* (although the property need not belong to another) but requiring in addition a further mental element.

---

**KEY PRINCIPLE:** *The intent (or recklessness) must be that the damage or destruction of the property be the cause of the danger to life.*

## R. v. Steer 1987

The victims were looking out of their bedroom window when the defendant shot at the window. He was charged with, inter alia, criminal damage with intent to endanger their lives or being reckless as to whether their lives would be endangered. His appeal was allowed by the Court of Appeal and the Crown appealed.

**HELD:** (H.L.) Appeal dismissed. It was not enough to show that the defendant intentionally or recklessly damaged property and intended that life be endangered or was reckless thereto. It was necessary to show that the intent was to endanger life *by* the damage or that the recklessness was as to whether life would be endangered *by* the damage. Here, the danger was caused by the shot and not by the damage to the property and so the defendant was rightly acquitted. [1987] 2 All E.R. 833

**KEY PRINCIPLE:** *In considering "Caldwell recklessness" as to endangerment of life, the test is whether the ordinary bystander would perceive an obvious risk of endangerment at the time of the damage or destruction.*

### R. v. Sangha 1988
(see p. 109)

**HELD:** (C.A.) Defendant's appeal dismissed. The relevant time for establishing recklessness was when the furniture was set alight. At that time, the ordinary prudent man would realise an obvious risk of life being endangered. The reasonable person was not endowed with "expert knowledge" (about, for example, the construction of the flats) nor with "the benefit of hindsight". [1988] 2 All E.R. 385

**COMMENTARY**
This purely objective test is the same as in the cases cited under section 1(1). Presumably however, defendants holding themselves out to be experts are tested on this basis.

# 11. INCHOATE OFFENCES

## Incitement

**KEY PRINCIPLE:** *Incitement requires persuasion or encouragement and more than mere suggestion.*

### R. v. Fitzmaurice 1983
The defendant encouraged B to commit a robbery, described as a "wages snatch", from a woman carrying money from her place of work to a bank in Bow. Unknown to either party, the plan was fictitious. The defendant was convicted of inciting B to

commit robbery and appealed against the direction on the meaning of incitement.

**HELD:** (C.A.) Appeal dismissed. The direction clearly drew attention to the element of persuasion needed for incitement. Because B was in need of money and was being offered reward for taking part, accompanying the suggestion by the implied promise of payment established the requisite persuasion. [1983] Q.B. 1083

## COMMENTARY
The second ground of appeal (impossibility) is dealt with below.

---

**KEY PRINCIPLE:** *The defendant must incite another to commit a crime.*

## R. v. Whitehouse 1977
The defendant pleaded guilty to inciting his 15-year old daughter to commit incest with him.

**HELD:** (C.A.) Appeal against conviction allowed. *Sexual Offences Act 1956*, s.11 establishes that a girl under the age of 16 is not capable in law of committing incest. Therefore, although there had been an incitement to engage in conduct, that conduct was not a crime by the girl and therefore there was no incitement to commit a crime. [1977] 1 Q.B. 868

## COMMENTARY
The prosecution tried to avoid the difficulty by alleging incitement of the girl to aid and abet the man to commit incest on her. However, this fell foul of the principle in *R. v. Tyrrell* (1894) (see p. 000). Since the girl belonged to the class protected by the existence of the offence, she could not be guilty of aiding and abetting the offence. Therefore, to incite her to do so was not criminal. The principle from *Whitehouse* remains good law although the activity involved is now criminal by virtue of *Criminal Law Act 1977*, s. 54.

---

**KEY PRINCIPLE:** *A defendant who belongs to a class protected by the existence of an offence cannot be guilty of inciting another to commit that offence against him or herself.*

# R. v. Tyrrell 1894

The defendant was convicted of inciting the crime of having sex with her whilst she was under 16.

**HELD:** (C.C.C.R.): Defendant's appeal allowed. Since the purpose of the crime was to protect the girl it could not also lead to her being punished for an offence committed on herself. [1894] I Q.B. 710

## COMMENTARY

The same decision was reached on aiding and abetting the offence (see Chapter 12). The principle is limited to crimes where the person falls within the specific class protected by the crime.

---

**KEY PRINCIPLE:** *A defendant cannot be guilty of incitement if the person incited lacks the* mens rea *of the offence incited.*

# R. v. Curr 1968

The defendant solicited women to obtain family allowance payments on his behalf and was convicted of the equivalent of inciting them to commit offences under section 9(b) of the *Family Allowance Act 1945*. He appealed on the basis that this required proof that the women knew they were not entitled to receive the money.

**HELD:** (D.C.) Appeal allowed. The offence incited required proof of *mens rea*. Even though the defendant knew the receipt was unlawful it was necessary to prove that the women also knew this in order to convict the defendant of incitement. [1968] 2 Q.B 944

## COMMENTARY

If the women lacked *mens rea*, the defendant was guilty of the offence through the innocent agency of the women. However, he was charged with incitement instead which, apparently, required proof that the women had *mens rea*. This has been criticised on the basis that it is the inciter's *mens rea* that is relevant and not that of the person incited. Also see *R. v. Shaw* (1994) which suggests that the *mens rea* of inciting theft is the same as for theft. This has also be criticised on the basis that the mens rea of incitement is not necessarily the same as the mens rea of the full offence.

---

**KEY PRINCIPLE:** *Impossibility may be a defence to inciting a specific course of conduct but not to inciting a general course of conduct.*

## R. v. Fitzmaurice 1983

(see p. 110). The second ground of the defendant's appeal was that the incited offence (being fictitious) was impossible to commit.

**HELD:** (C.A.) Dismissing the appeal. Since incitement is a common law offence, impossibility is governed by *D.P.P. v. Nock & Alsford* (1978) (see p. 124). It is therefore necessary to distinguish between a persuasion in general terms and one that is directed to a specific crime and target. The former is not defeated by impossibility whilst the latter is. However on the facts of the instant case, inciting "a robbery of a woman at Bow" was not impossible and so the issue did not arise. [1983] Q.B. 1083

# Attempt

**KEY PRINCIPLE:** *The* actus reus *of attempt is not established if the defendant is merely preparing to commit a crime.*

## R. v. Gullefer 1990

The defendant tried to distract greyhounds because the dog he had backed was losing. He intended to cause the race to be abandoned so that he could recover his stake. He was convicted of attempted theft.

**HELD:** (C.A.) Defendant's appeal allowed. There was insufficient evidence that the defendant had passed beyond mere preparation to steal. [1990] 3 All E.R. 882

## R. v. Campbell 1991

The defendant, who admitted intending to rob a post office, was arrested just outside the post office door. He had been observed earlier "lurking around" the post office in motor cycle gear and wearing sunglasses as a form of disguise. He had in his possession a threatening note and imitation firearm. He was convicted of attempted robbery and appealed.

**HELD:** (C.A.) Appeal allowed. The acts undertaken were mere preparation. (1991) 93 Cr. App. R 350

## COMMENTARY
The court took the view that whilst each case was to be decided on its own facts, it was unlikely that a person could be said to have committed an attempt if he had not even "gained the place where he could . . . carry out the offence".

---

**KEY PRINCIPLE:** *The actus reus of attempt is established if the defendant has done an act that is more than merely preparatory to the commission of the full offence.*

## R. v. Jones 1990
The defendant bought guns, shortened one barrel and test-fired them. He packed various weapons in his bag and drove to where the victim was dropping his child at school. He got into the victim's car and asked him to drive, pointing at him the loaded sawn-off shotgun (with its safety catch on). The victim grabbed the gun and threw it out of the car. The defendant was convicted of attempted murder and appealed on the basis that there was no attempt because he had still to remove the safety catch from the gun, put his finger on the trigger and pull it before the full offence could be committed.

**HELD:** (C.A.) Appeal dismissed. Whilst the acts up to and including arrival at the school were only preparatory, getting into the car and pointing the gun was sufficient evidence of attempt. [1990] 1 W.L.R. 1057

---

**KEY PRINCIPLE:** *"More than mere preparation" is a question of fact and reference should no longer be made to the old tests for establishing "proximity".*

## R. v. Gullefer 1990
(see p. 113).

**HELD:** (C.A.) The judge determines whether there is any evidence of acts going beyond mere preparation but if there is any such evidence it is for the jury to decide whether the defendant did so in fact.

## COMMENTARY

The court decided that it was not relevant to refer to the law prior to the Criminal Attempts Act 1981. In any event, the "old" last act test was no longer appropriate, nor was it necessary to show that the defendant had reached a point from which he could not retreat. The same approach was adopted in *Campbell* and *Jones* where the court rejected the defence argument that "more than merely preparatory" meant "the last act". The court said that the natural meaning of the statutory words should be adopted rather than earlier case law.

---

**KEY PRINCIPLE:** *The* mens rea *of attempt requires proof that the defendant intended to bring about any results specified in the full offence.*

## R. v. Whybrow 1951

The defendant connected an electrical device to a bath, causing his wife to receive an electric shock. He was convicted of attempted murder and appealed against the direction that intention to cause grievous bodily harm was sufficient *mens rea* for attempted murder.

**HELD:** (C.A.) Appeal dismissed. There had been a misdirection but no miscarriage of justice. Whilst murder is satisfied by proof of intent to cause grievous bodily harm, attempted murder is only satisfied by proof of intention to bring about the full offence (*i.e.* intention to kill). (1951) 35 Cr. App. R. 141

## COMMENTARY

The case illustrates that the *mens rea* of attempt can be more stringent than that of the full offence. Whilst the case is decided on the common law, the same principle applies to statutory attempt: *R. v. Millard & Vernon* (1987) (see p. 116).

---

**KEY PRINCIPLE:** *Even where the full offence is satisfied by proof of recklessness in respect of a result, attempting the offence requires proof of intent.*

# R. v. Millard & Vernon 1987

The defendants were convicted of attempted criminal damage on a direction that recklessness as to the risk of damage was sufficient.

**HELD:** (C.A.) Defendant's appeal allowed. The *Criminal Attempts Act 1981* requires proof of intent to commit the full offence. This is the position even where the substantive offence is satisfied by proof of recklessness in respect of a result such as "damage" in the case of criminal damage. [1987] Crim.L.R. 393

## COMMENTARY

Even prior to *Moloney* (see Chapter 2, p. 15), attempt required proof of direct intent (aim/purpose) in respect of results: *R. v. Mohan* (1976). Foresight was not equivalent to intent. The same is true under the Act: *R. v. Pearman* (1984) although foresight that the result is virtually certain is evidence of intent: *Walker & Hayles* (1990) (see Chapter 2, p. 17).

---

**KEY PRINCIPLE:** *Where the full offence is satisfied by recklessness in respect of elements (other than any specified result), recklessness in respect of those elements is also sufficient for attempting the offence.*

# R. v. Khan 1990

The defendants were convicted of attempted rape on a direction that recklessness as to lack of consent was sufficient *mens rea*. They appealed on the basis that attempt required proof of intent.

**HELD:** (C.A.) Appeal dismissed. The words "with intent to commit an offence" in *Criminal Attempts Act 1981*, s.1 only apply to intent to do the act and to cause any results. Therefore, attempted rape requires proof of an intent to have sexual intercourse. However, since recklessness as to lack of consent is sufficient for the full offence, the same is true for attempting the offence. [1990] 1 W.L.R. 813

# Attorney-General's Reference (No. 3 of 1992) 1994

The defendants were acquitted of attempted aggravated arson, being reckless as to whether life would be endangered on a ruling that intent to endanger life had to be proven.

**HELD:** (C.A.) Intent had to be proven in respect of the result specified in the full offence (damage or destruction) but since recklessness in relation to endangerment of life was sufficient for the full offence it was also sufficient for attempting the offence. [1994] 2 All E.R. 121

## COMMENTARY
The court also held that the *Caldwell* definition of recklessness applied as it did for the full offence. Where recklessness is not sufficient for the full offence, knowledge must be established for attempting the offence.

---

**KEY PRINCIPLE:** *Impossibility is no defence to a charge of attempting an offence.*

# R. v. Shivpuri 1987

The defendant was convicted of attempt to be knowingly involved in dealing with a prohibited drug, having received a suitcase which he mistakenly believed to contain drugs. He appealed on the basis that, *inter alia*, impossibility provided a defence to the charge.

**HELD:** (H.L.) Appeal dismissed. Since the defendant had the *mens rea* and had committed the *actus reus* of the attempt, he was guilty because *Criminal Attempts Act 1981*, s.1(2) provides that impossibility is no defence. The earlier House of Lords decision in *Anderton v. Ryan* (1985) was overruled. [1987] A.C. 1

## COMMENTARY
The House of Lords decided in *Haughton* v. *Smith* (1975) that legal impossibility was a defence to attempt (*ratio*) as was physical impossibility (*obiter*). *Criminal Attempts Act 1981*, s.1(2) states that "a person may be guilty of attempting to commit an offence . . . even though the facts are such that the commission of the offence is impossible." Nevertheless, in *Anderton v. Ryan*, the House decided that Mrs Ryan was not guilty of attempting to handle a stolen video recorder

when it could not be proven that it had been stolen. They decided that section 1(2) merely abolished the defence of physical (or factual) impossibility but had not affected cases of legal impossibility. *Shivpuri* overrules this (although it could be distinguished because *Shivpuri* intended to commit an offence—importing drugs, whilst Mrs Ryan did not—she merely intended to buy a cheap video recorder). Lord Bridge stated that reasons given to explain *Anderton* (the "doctrine" of "objective innocence" and that of "dominant intention") were not to be used. In particular, the latter contradicted s.1(3) of the Act which provides that a defendant's intention is to be judged by reference to the facts as s/he believed them to be.

# Conspiracy: Statutory

**KEY PRINCIPLE:** *The defendant must have agreed with one or more persons that "a course of conduct shall be pursued".*

## R. v. Anderson 1986

The defendant agreed to participate in the planned escape of a prisoner. He intended to obtain wire cutting equipment to be smuggled into the prison but claimed to intend to take no further part in the scheme. He appealed against conviction for statutory conspiracy on the basis of lack of mens rea.

**HELD:** (H.L.) In dismissing the appeal for reasons given below, Lord Bridge analysed the elements of the offence. The first element was that there must be an agreement between two or more persons to pursue a course of conduct. [1986] A.C. 27

**COMMENTARY**
Section 1(1) of the *Criminal Law Act 1977* which replaces most of the common law of conspiracy sets out this requirement, which is the same as for common law conspiracy. The way in which the offences differ relates to the nature of course of conduct agreed upon. Where there are only two parties to the agreement, there are certain situations where no liability arises because, for example, the parties are spouses, or one is a minor or the victim of the intended offence.

**KEY PRINCIPLE:** *The conspiracy is statutory, where the course of conduct agreed upon would, if carried out, amount to or involve one of the agreeing parties in the commission of an offence.*

## R. v. Ayres 1984

The defendant agreed to defraud an insurance company by falsely claiming that an insured vehicle and its contents were stolen. The defendant was charged and convicted of common law conspiracy to defraud. He appealed on the basis that the conspiracy was to commit *Theft Act 1968*, s.15 and so should have been charged as statutory conspiracy.

**HELD:** (H.L.) Appeal dismissed. The charge was incorrectly laid but no miscarriage of justice occurred. The *Criminal Law Act 1977* provides that agreements that necessarily involve or amount to the commission of an offence by one or more of the conspirators are statutory conspiracies. [1984] 1 A.C. 447

**COMMENTARY**
The House held that statutory and common law conspiracy were mutually exclusive but this is no longer the case: *Criminal Justice Act 1987*, s.12. An agreement to become an accomplice to an offence may not amount to a statutory conspiracy (since being an accomplice does not amount to a crime as such). In *R. v. Hollinshead* (1985) (H.L.), an agreement to manufacture and sell devices which enabled purchasers to defraud the electricity board amounted to a common law conspiracy to defraud but did not disclose a statutory conspiracy. This may support the view that agreements to become an accomplice do not fall within statutory conspiracy. However, alternatively, it was simply that there was insufficient evidence of an agreement to aid, abet, counsel or procure the purchaser's fraud.

---

**KEY PRINCIPLE:** *Only planned consequences fall within the agreed course of conduct.*

## R. v. Siracusa 1990

The defendant was charged with a conspiracy to import heroin from Thailand and another conspiracy to import cannabis from Kashmir. The defendant appealed against, *inter alia*, a direction on the mens rea of the conspiracies charged.

**HELD:** (C.A.) Appeal dismissed. If conspiracy to import heroin is charged, the prosecution must prove that the agreed course of conduct was to do precisely this and not merely to import a drug. Although the full offence is committed even where the defendant believes the drug to be of a different class, a conspiracy to import heroin (Class A drug) cannot be established by proving an agreement to import cannabis (Class B drug) or vice versa. (1990) 90 Cr. App. R. 340

## COMMENTARY

(1) The court noted that, facts allowing, it was acceptable under the 1977 Act to charge just one conspiracy to import prohibited drugs of more than one class.

(2) Only intended consequences fall within the scope of the conspiracy and at least two of the conspirators must know of any circumstances that are specified in the full offence. Recklessness is not sufficient.

---

**KEY PRINCIPLE:** *A defendant does not have to intend to play an active part in the agreed course of conduct.*

# R. v. Siracusa 1990

(see above).

**HELD:** (C.A.) Because participation in a conspiracy varies, knowledge of "what was going on", combined with an intention to participate in the agreement that others will further the criminal purpose is sufficient. (1990) 90 Cr. App. R. 340

## COMMENTARY

Simply intending that others continue with the planned course of conduct, with knowledge that this involves the commission of an offence, is apparently sufficient. Problems were caused by the statement of Lord Bridge in *Anderson* that the *mens rea* of conspiracy required proof that the accused "intended to play some part in the agreed course of conduct in furtherance of the criminal purpose". The court in *Siracusa* explained that this did not mean "play some active part" but could be established in the way indicated.

---

**KEY PRINCIPLE:** *The course of conduct must necessarily amount to or involve a crime if the agreement were carried out in accordance with the intentions of the conspirators.*

# R. v. Anderson 1986

(see p. 118).

**HELD:** (H.L.) Defendant's appeal dismissed. The *mens rea* of conspiracy did not require proof that each conspirator intended the agreement be carried out. Therefore, since the defendant intended to play some part in the agreed course of conduct, he was guilty even though he did not intend that the plan be carried out. [1986] A.C. 27

**COMMENTARY**
Lord Bridge did not take the 1977 Act to mean that the conspirators had to intend the agreement to be carried out. Nevertheless, he wished to ensure an acquittal for persons entering a conspiracy without any intention of playing a part to bring about the agreed course of conduct (such as those entering with intention to frustrate the conspiracy). This point arose in *Yip Chiu-Cheung v. R.* (1994). The defendant agreed to import drugs with a person who unknown to him was a drug enforcement officer who entered the agreement in order to arrange for the arrest of the participants. Relying on the *obiter* in *Anderson*, the defendant argued that there was no conspiracy. The Privy Council held that the case fell outside the exception envisaged by Lord Bridge because, the drug enforcement officer did intend to take part in the planned crime (albeit intending to frustrate it). However, there may be a conflict between *Yip* and *Anderson* because the former stated that "the crime . . . requires an agreement . . . with the intention of carrying it out." Yet, *Anderson* seems to suggest the opposite. The fact that *Yip* is a case of common law conspiracy is not sufficient to distinguish the cases.

---

**KEY PRINCIPLE:** *An agreement conditional upon a contingency arising may still be a conspiracy.*

# R. v. Jackson 1985

The defendants were convicted of conspiracy to pervert the course of justice by agreeing to injure their co-defendant if he was convicted at trial. They appealed on the basis that their agreement would not 'necessarily' amount to or involve the commission of an offence (as required by *Criminal Law Act 1977*, s.1) because the offence would only be committed if the "victim" was convicted.

**HELD:** (C.A.) Appeal dismissed. If the contingency arose, carrying out the plan would give rise to the commission of an offence. "Necessarily" did not mean inevitably. [1985] Crim.L.R. 442

**COMMENTARY**
Contrast the example given by Donaldson LJ in the case of *Reed* (1982)

# Conspiracy: Common Law

**KEY PRINCIPLE:** *Common law conspiracy to defraud consists of agreeing to dishonestly deprive another of something (including injury to a proprietary right) or to dishonestly cause a public officer to act in contravention of duty.*

## R. v. Scott 1975

The defendants were convicted of conspiracy to defraud by agreeing to borrow, copy and distribute films in breach of copyright. They appealed on the basis that they had not agreed to deceive anyone (such as the copyright owners).

**HELD:** (H.L.) Appeal dismissed. A conspiracy to defraud could arise without deception or deceit. To defraud was "to deprive a person of something which is his or to which he is or would or might be entitled and . . . to injure some proprietary right of his . . ." It was also possible to commit the offence without financial advantage being gained or loss caused. [1975] A.C. 819

**COMMENTARY**
The court also recognised conspiracy to defraud involved in deceiving public officers to act contrary to their duty. The offence requires proof of intention to defraud and dishonesty but not intent to cause economic loss. Common law conspiracy to defraud is preserved by *Criminal Law Act 1977*, s.5(2); and *Criminal Justice Act 1987*, s.12 provides that this may be charged even where the agreement is also a statutory conspiracy.

**KEY PRINCIPLE:** *Conspiracy to corrupt public morals exists at common law where the conduct agreed upon would not amount to an offence by an individual if carried out.*

## Shaw v. DPP 1962

The defendants published a "Ladies Directory" containing the contact details of prostitutes. They were convicted of, *inter alia*, conspiracy to corrupt public morals.

**HELD:** (H.L.) Defendant's appeal dismissed. The offence of conspiracy to corrupt public morals existed at common law. This might include conduct that was not in itself illegal but was calculated to corrupt the public morality. The jury were the arbitrators of what corrupted public morals. [1962] A.C. 220

### COMMENTARY
The existence of the offence was confirmed in *Knuller v. D.P.P.* (1973) (see below) and is preserved by *Criminal Law Act 1977*, s.5(3)(a). "Corrupting public morals" has been described as something that the jury considers to be "destructive of the very fabric of society": Lord Simon in *Knuller*.

---

**KEY PRINCIPLE:** *Conspiracy to outrage public decency exists at common law where the conduct agreed upon would not amount to an offence by an individual if carried out.*

## Knuller v. DPP 1973

The defendants published a magazine with advertisements for homosexual contacts. They appealed against conviction of conspiracy to corrupt public morals and conspiracy to outrage public decency.

**HELD:** (H.L.) Appeal dismissed in relation to conspiracy to corrupt public morals and allowed in respect of conspiracy to outrage public decency. A bare majority concluded that the latter offence existed at common law but there had been a misdirection on its elements. "To outrage" meant more than "to offend" or "to disgust" and public "decency" was a shifting standard. Moreover, according to Lord Simon, "public" decency means that the offence must be committed in public. [1973] A.C. 435

**COMMENTARY**
This offence is also preserved by *Criminal Law Act 1977*, s.5(3)(b).

---

**KEY PRINCIPLE:** *Impossibility is a defence to common law conspiracy to engage in a specific course of conduct.*

## D.P.P. v. Nock & Alsford 1978

The defendants were convicted of conspiracy to produce cocaine. They agreed to obtain cocaine from a particular powder in their possession which, unknown to them, would not produce cocaine.

**HELD:** (H.L.) Defendant's appeal allowed. Since the agreement was limited to engaging in a specific course of conduct from which it was impossible to commit the full offence, the defendants were not guilty. The answer might differ if the agreement had been of a general nature (for example, to go into the business of cocaine production) because this agreement would not be rendered impossible just because one powder would not yield cocaine. [1978] A.C. 979

**COMMENTARY**
Whilst this decision still represents the position at common law, statutory conspiracies are governed by *Criminal Attempts Act 1981*, s.5 which provides that impossibility is no defence.

---

# 12. PARTIES

## Accomplices

**KEY PRINCIPLE:** *An accomplice is one who aids, abets, counsels or procures the commission of an offence.*

## Attorney-General's Reference (No. 1 of 1975)

(see p. 126).

**HELD:** (C.A.) Liability as an accomplice (secondary party) arises by aiding, abetting, counselling or procuring and these words probably differ in meaning. [1975] 1 Q.B. 773

**KEY PRINCIPLE:** *Aiding and abetting requires proof of more than non-accidental presence. There must, in addition, be actual agreement, encouragement or assistance.*

## R. v. Clarkson & Carroll 1971

The defendants watched a rape but there was no evidence that they agreed to or positively assisted in the crime. They were convicted of rape as aiders and abettors and appealed.

**HELD:** (C.M.A.C.) Appeal allowed. In the absence of prior agreement or positive physical assistance, mere presence was insufficient without actual encouragement and intention to encourage. [1971] 1 W.L.R. 1402

**COMMENTARY**
The court felt that mere presence might, in some circumstances, provide evidence of encouragement and intention to encourage. The next case is an example.

---

**KEY PRINCIPLE:** *Evidence of encouragement may arise from a failure to prevent an offence if the defendant had a right to control the principal offender.*

## Du Cros v. Lambourne 1907

The owner of a car was convicted of driving at a dangerous speed, having failed to prevent the driver from doing so.

**HELD:** (D.C.) Defendant's appeal dismissed. As owner, he could and should have stopped the driver. Failing to do so when he had a right of control was evidence that he encouraged and approved the activity. [1907] 1 K.B. 40

**COMMENTARY**
Likewise, failing to act in breach of a duty to do so may provide evidence of aiding and abetting: *R. v. Forman & Ford* (1988) (see p. 128).

---

**KEY PRINCIPLE:** *Counselling requires consensus but not causation. It is sufficient that the principal acts within the scope of the counselling.*

## R. v. Calhaem 1985

The defendant was charged with murder as counsellor and procurer, having hired a private detective to kill the victim. The detective did so, but in circumstances that suggested no substantial causal link between the counselling and the killing.

**HELD:** (C.A.) Defendant's appeal dismissed. The word 'counsel' does not imply a causal connection. There must simply be contact between the offenders and a connection between the counselling and the offence. Since the killing was done within the scope of the counselling, liability was established. [1985] 1 Q.B. 808

---

**KEY PRINCIPLE:** *Procuring does not require consensus but there must be a causal link between the offence and the procuring.*

## Attorney-General's Reference (No. 1 of 1975)

The defendant surreptitiously laced a friend's drink, knowing that he was about to drive. He was charged with driving with excess alcohol as an accomplice and acquitted on the basis that there was no meeting of minds between principal and accomplice.

**HELD:** (C.A.) Whilst aiding, abetting and counselling probably require consensus, the same was not true of procuring. Procuring "means to produce by endeavour . . . setting out to see that it happens and taking appropriate steps to produce (it)." There must be a causal link in the sense that the offence would not have been committed in the absence of the procuring. Therefore the facts did raise a case of procuring. [1975] 1 Q.B. 773

---

**KEY PRINCIPLE:** *An accomplice must intend to aid, abet, counsel or procure the offence. This is satisfied by proof of voluntary involvement with knowledge of the circumstances.*

## National Coal Board v. Gamble 1959

A weighbridge operator issued a weight ticket to a driver, knowing that the lorry would be driven overweight. The defendants appealed against conviction on the basis of lack of *mens rea*.

**HELD:** (D.C.) Appeal dismissed. Supplying "the instrument for a crime or anything essential to its commission" amounts to aiding and abetting if done knowingly with intent to aid and abet. Proof of intent only requires an act of involvement voluntarily done. [1959] 1 Q.B. 11

### COMMENTARY
Intent does not mean desire or purpose and liability arises even where the accomplice is indifferent about the commission of the offence. Contrast *R. v. Clarke* (1985) where it was held that participation with the sole motive of frustrating an offence did not amount to aiding and abetting.

---

**KEY PRINCIPLE:** *An accomplice must have more than a general criminal intention but need not know the details of the offence to be committed.*

## R. v. Bainbridge 1960
The defendant was convicted as an accomplice, having supplied cutting equipment, knowing that it would be used for breaking and entering. He appealed on the basis that he did not know sufficient details of the planned offence to be an accomplice.

**HELD:** (C.C.A.) Appeal dismissed. A defendant who only knows that an "illegal venture" is planned does not have sufficient *mens rea*. However, one who knows that a crime of the type in question is planned does have sufficient *mens rea* even though the details are not known. [1960] 1 Q.B. 129

---

**KEY PRINCIPLE:** *It is not necessary that the accomplice knows the type of crime to be committed as long as the crime falls within the range of crimes contemplated.*

## D.P.P. for Northern Ireland v. Maxwell 1978
A member of the U.V.F. was convicted in respect of driving to a planned bombing. He appealed on the basis that he did not know the nature of the activity to be carried out by the principals.

**HELD:** (H.L.) Appeal dismissed. Whilst the defendant did not know precisely what form the attack would take, he did contemplate a limited number of offences (including shooting, bombing and the use of an incendiary device). He was therefore guilty of whichever of these contemplated crimes actually occurred. [1978] 3 All E.R. 1140

## COMMENTARY
Viscount Dilhorne and Lord Scarman rejected the criteria used in *Bainbridge* because liability should not rest on categorising activities into types of crimes.

---

**KEY PRINCIPLE:** *It is not necessary to prove which party was principal and which was accomplice if the crime is committed in the course of a joint enterprise.*

## R. v. Forman & Ford 1988
The victim was assaulted by one of two police officers in a cell. The defence submitted that, without evidence that the parties were acting in concert, the failure to identify who actually did the act was fatal.

**HELD:** (Cr. Ct.) Submission rejected. If it cannot be proved which party committed the assault, both must be acquitted unless there is evidence of joint enterprise in the sense that one did the act relying on the other's encouragement not to intervene or report the offence. [1988] Crim.L.R. 677

## COMMENTARY
It was similarly stated in *Chan Wing-Siu v. R.* (1985) (see p. 130) that the prosecution does not have to prove who was principal or accomplice if the offence arises in the course of a pre-arranged plan or concerted action (joint enterprise).

---

**KEY PRINCIPLE:** *If the principal deliberately acts outside the scope of a joint enterprise, the accomplice is not liable for those acts.*

## R. v. Anderson & Morris 1966
The principal was convicted of murder, having stabbed the victim with intent. The accomplice was convicted of manslaughter on a direction that he could be guilty even if the use of the knife was without his knowledge and outside the common design.

**HELD:** (C.C.A.) Defendant's appeal allowed. If one party "goes beyond what has been tacitly agreed as part of the common enterprise, his co-adventurer is not liable for the consequences of that unauthorised act." [1966] 2 Q.B. 110

## COMMENTARY
The position differs where the act occurs within the scope of the joint enterprise. This means that careful attention must be given to the precise nature of that enterprise (see p. 000).

---

**KEY PRINCIPLE:** *An accomplice is only liable for unforseen consequences arising out of a joint enterprise to the same extent as a principal.*

## R. v. Anderson & Morris 1966
(see p. 128).

**HELD:** (C.C.A.) In cases of joint enterprise "each is liable for acts done in pursuance of that joint enterprise . . . that includes liability for unusual consequences if they arise from the execution of the agreed joint enterprise." It was for a jury to decide whether the act fell within the enterprise or went beyond it. [1966] 2 Q.B. 110

## COMMENTARY
(1) If the principal acts within the enterprise, an accomplice may be liable for the consequences. Where the offence arising out of the activity requires proof of *mens rea*, the accomplice must foresee the consequence. However, where liability can arise for unforeseen consequences (for example, manslaughter), the accomplice may be liable on this basis. Likewise, the doctrine of transferred malice applies so that where the offence is accidentally committed against the wrong victim, the accomplice (like the principal) can be guilty. The position differs if the wrong victim is deliberately chosen by the principal because the action is then outside the joint enterprise.
(2) To illustrate the importance of determining whether the activity is within or outside the joint enterprise, compare *R. v. O'Brien* (1995) and *Chan Wing-Siu* (see p. 130) with *R. v. Perman* (1995). In *O'Brien*, the accomplice knew that the principal might use a loaded rifle and so was guilty of attempted murder when the principal used it in the course of their enter-

prise. In *Perman*, the accomplice thought that the principal had an unloaded gun to frighten anyone who intervened in a robbery. In fact, the gun was loaded and the principal killed during the robbery. The accomplice was not guilty of manslaughter because, by using a loaded gun, the principal had acted outside the scope of the enterprise, which was limited to robbery with an unloaded gun. This is similar to *Anderson* but the outcome would differ (as in the next case) if the principal had somehow killed by using an unloaded gun (acting within the enterprise).

---

**KEY PRINCIPLE:** *Accomplices are liable for crimes arising in the course of a joint enterprise to the extent of their own mens rea.*

## Chan Wing-Siu v. R. 1985

The defendants were convicted of, *inter alia*, murder occurring in the course of a joint enterprise (armed robbery). The defendants appealed against conviction on the basis that they could only be liable if they foresaw death or grievous bodily harm would probably result.

**HELD:** (P.C.) Appeal dismissed. Liability arose because the acts occurred within the joint enterprise. Whether the liability was for murder or manslaughter depended on what the accomplice contemplated. If they thought that weapons would only be used to frighten, the crime was manslaughter. If they contemplated that they might be used to kill or cause grievous bodily harm, the crime was murder. It was not necessary that this was foreseen as more probable than not. Foreseeing that it might happen was sufficient. [1985] 1 A.C. 168

**COMMENTARY**
(1) It is not necessary to show that the accomplice intended death or grievous bodily harm for liability to arise for murder. It is sufficient that s/he realises that the principal might act with this intent.
(2) Because liability rests on each party's contemplation, an accomplice can be convicted of a more (or less) serious offence than the principal in respect of the same activity: confirmed in *R. v. Howe* (1987) (see Chapter 14, p. 151).

---

**KEY PRINCIPLE:** *An accomplice can only be convicted if the actus reus of the principal offence is committed.*

## Thornton v. Mitchell 1940

A bus driver was acquitted of negligent driving but the bus conductor (who was negligent) was convicted as an accomplice.

**HELD:** (D.C.) Defendant's appeal allowed. If the driver had not driven negligently there was no act that the conductor could be said to have aided and abetted. [1940] 1 All E.R. 339

**KEY PRINCIPLE:** *An accomplice can be convicted even though the principal is acquitted.*

## R. v. Cogan & Leak 1976

Leak procured Cogan to have sexual intercourse with Mrs Leak without her consent. Cogan was acquitted of rape because the jury accepted that he believed Mrs Leak was consenting. Leak appealed against his conviction for rape as an aider and abettor on the basis of Cogan's acquittal.

**HELD:** (C.A.) Appeal dismissed. The *actus reus* of rape had taken place and that was sufficient to convict an accomplice. It was no defence for Leak that Cogan was acquitted due to lack of *mens rea*. [1976] 1 Q.B. 217

### COMMENTARY

The same principle applies where the accomplice has committed the actus reus but has a defence. A further example can be found in *R. v. Wheelhouse* (1994) (C.A.) where the principal was acquitted of burglary (because of lack of *mens rea*) whilst the accomplice was guilty as procurer.

**KEY PRINCIPLE:** *A person who uses an innocent agent to commit the offence is guilty as principal offender.*

## R. v. Cogan & Leak 1976

(see above).

**HELD:** (C.A.) In the course of dismissing the appeal, Lawton LJ indicated that Leak could have been indicted as a principal using Cogan (an innocent agent) as the means to procure the offence. [1976] 1 Q.B. 217

**COMMENTARY**

This part of the judgement has been criticised on the basis that rape is an offence requiring personal action and cannot be committed by an agent. The same problem does not arise with offences like theft and burglary where personal action is not specified. Thus, in *Wheelhouse*, the defendant could have been guilty as a principal acting through the innocent agency of the person he procured to commit the offence for him.

---

**KEY PRINCIPLE:** *An accomplice may avoid liability by effective withdrawal from the enterprise.*

## R. v. Becerra 1975

The principal committed murder in the course of a joint enterprise to use force during a burglary if necessary. One ground for appeal against conviction as an accomplice was that the defendant had withdrawn from the joint enterprise before the killing occurred.

**HELD:** (C.A.) Application dismissed. The defendant simply said "let's go" and then ran away just before the killing. Effective withdrawal varies according to the circumstances. By the time this defendant withdrew, he would have had to "repent" in a vastly different and more effective manner (by, for example, physically intervening to stop the stabbing or by warning the victim). (1975) 62 Cr.App.R. 212

**COMMENTARY**

Where possible, communication of withdrawal should be timely and give unequivocal notice that assistance and aid are withdrawn. So, in *R. v. Baker* (1994) (C.A.), saying 'I'm not doing it', passing a weapon back to another, and remaining at the scene was neither unequivocal nor effective withdrawal.

---

**KEY PRINCIPLE:** *A person falling within the class for whose protection the offence exists cannot be an accomplice to it.*

## R. v. Tyrrell 1894

(see Chapter 11, p. 112).

**HELD:** (C.C.C.R.) For the same reason that the girl could not be guilty of inciting under age sex against herself nor could she be an accomplice to it. [1894] 1 Q.B. 710

**COMMENTARY**

The same issue was raised in Whitehouse (1977) (see Chapter 11, p. 000). However, a person who is a victim in a looser sense can be an accomplice to the crime involved.

# Vicarious Liability

**KEY PRINCIPLE:** *The language and object of some offences enables vicarious liability to arise for the acts of an agent or servant acting in the course of employment.*

## Coppen v. Moore (No. 2) 1898

Despite contrary instruction from the employer, goods were sold by false description. The employer was liable vicariously.

**HELD:** (D.C.) Defendant's appeal dismissed. The effect of the relevant statute was to make masters or principals criminally liable for the acts of servants or agents committed within the scope of their employment. The defendant had therefore sold the goods through his servants. [1898] 2 Q.B. 306

**COMMENTARY**

(1) The "language, scope and object" of the statute enabled the imposition of vicarious liability which arose even though the acts were unauthorised. Other words that can be similarly construed include "use", "supply", "present" and "keep". *Mens rea* words cannot be extensively construed and so this principle can only be used for strict liability offences.

(2) The parties must, generally, be master and servant or agent and the act must occur in the scope of employment and not as a "frolic of the agent's own".

---

**KEY PRINCIPLE:** *A person who delegates the performance of their duty to another will be held responsible for the actions and states of mind of that other.*

## Allen v. Whitehead 1930

Contrary to the licensee's instructions, the manager of a cafe allowed prostitutes to gather on the premises. The licensee was convicted of an offence under the *Metropolitan Police Act 1839* which required proof of *mens rea*.

**HELD:** (D.C.) Since the defendant was absent from the premises and had delegated to a manager, that manager's acts and knowledge were imputed to the defendant. [1930] 1 K.B. 211

## COMMENTARY
In reaching this conclusion, the court looked to the purpose of the Act and concluded that it would be rendered nugatory if licensees could avoid liability by absenting themselves from premises by appointing a delegate.

---

**KEY PRINCIPLE:** *Whether delegation has taken place is a question of fact, requiring evidence of the transfer of authority.*

## Vane v. Yiannopoullos 1965
The licensee was in a restaurant basement when a sale in breach of license took place elsewhere without his knowledge. The sale was by a waitress and the licensee was originally found guilty of knowingly making the sale in breach of licence.

**HELD:** (H.L.) Prosecution appeal dismissed. There was insufficient evidence of delegation on the facts. The waitress had not been "left in charge of the premises", "all the effective management" had not been handed over. [1965] A.C. 486

## COMMENTARY
The House of Lords expressed distaste for the principle of delegation. The defendant was acquitted because the court felt that delegation required a transfer of the whole of one's authority to another and some felt that it was necessary that the licensee be absent from the premises. However, compare the next case.

## Howker v. Robinson 1973
A barman made an illegal sale whilst the licensee was in a different bar. The licensee was found guilty of the breach of licence and appealed.

**HELD:** (D.C.) Appeal dismissed. Delegation was a question of fact and since the barman had been given complete control over the lounge bar, effective delegation had occurred. [1973] 1 Q.B. 178

**COMMENTARY**
The decision was reached despite the presence of the licensee on the premises which the court said was not a conclusive factor. Moreover, delegation had taken place even though there had not been a transfer of all of the licensee's authority to the barman.

# Corporate Liability

**KEY PRINCIPLE:** *A corporation is identified with its controllers (directing mind and will) such that their actions and states of mind are those of the corporation.*

## Tesco v. Nattrass 1972

A supermarket manager was responsible for an offence under the *Trade Descriptions Act 1968*. The Company was charged and pleaded a defence under the Act that the manager was "another person" for whom they were not liable. Liability turned on whether the manager was a servant (another person) or someone with whom the corporation could be identified.

**HELD:** (H.L.) Defendant's appeal allowed. A corporation is vicariously liable for the acts of servants in the same way as a natural employer. However, where the acts (and states of mind) are those of "the directing mind and will" of the company, liability is not vicarious. These persons are identified with the corporation, so that their acts and states of mind are those of the corporation. Because of the management structure of Tesco Ltd, store managers were not such persons and their acts were not acts of the company itself. [1972] A.C. 153

**COMMENTARY**
The court referred to Denning LJ's description in *Bolton v. Graham* (1957) (C.A.) that the "brain and nerve centre" of a company are identified with it whilst the "hands" of the company are not. The court said that normally it was the board of directors, managing director and other superior officers who carry out management functions whose actions are identified with the company.

**KEY PRINCIPLE:** *Corporate liability can arise for manslaughter.*

### P & O European Ferries (Dover) Ltd 1991

On trial for manslaughter arising out of the sinking of the ferry, Herald of Free Enterprise, the question was whether a company could be liable for an offence such as manslaughter.

**HELD:** (Cr. Ct.) If the perpetrator of the offence was a human being with whom the corporation could be identified, liability could arise. (1991) 93 Cr.App.R. 72

#### COMMENTARY

Despite previous doubts, the case confirms that corporate manslaughter can arise under the doctrine of identification. Ultimately P & O were not liable because there was no evidence that a controlling officer had the requisite *mens rea*. Compare *R. v. OII Ltd* (1994) where a leisure company and its managing director were convicted of manslaughter in respect of the death of several canoeists in a trip organised by the company. Gross negligence existed in many aspects of the company activities and the director was identified with the company.

---

# 13. DEFENCES (1)

## Self-induced intoxication

**KEY PRINCIPLE:** *Self-induced (voluntary) intoxication can be used as evidence to disprove the mens rea of specific but not basic intent crimes.*

### D.P.P. v. Majewski 1977

The defendant attacked a number of people but claimed lack of *mens rea* due to self-induced intoxication through drink and drugs. He was convicted of a variety of assaults on a direction that self-induced intoxication was no defence.

**HELD:** (H.L.) Defendant's appeal dismissed. Where a crime requires proof of specific intent, lack of *mens rea* due to self-induced intoxication results in an acquittal. However, it is a substantive rule of law that self-induced intoxication is irrelevant and no defence to a crime of basic intent (such as assault). [1977] A.C. 443

**COMMENTARY**

(1) The principles only apply to voluntary or self-induced intoxication (described as an intoxicant "consciously and deliberately" taken) and only where lack of *mens rea* is pleaded. If *mens rea* exists despite intoxication, the defendant is guilty as charged.

(2) There is a major difficulty in satisfactorily defining specific and basic intent crimes. Approval was given to Lord Simon's definition (from *D.P.P. v. Morgan* (1976)): a basic intent crime is one whose definition specifies *mens rea* that "does not go beyond the *actus reus* . . . (the act and its consequences)". A specific (or ulterior) intent crime is one where the "*mens rea* goes beyond contemplation of the *actus reus*". It was also suggested in *Majewski* that a specific intent crime is one that requires proof of some "purposive element" and that a crime satisfied by proof of recklessness is one of basic intent. These definitions are not without difficulty. Examples of specific intent crimes given in *Majewski* were murder and s.18 *Offences Against the Person Act 1861* whilst assault, s.20, and manslaughter were crimes of basic intent.

(3) The court accepted that there was no logic in allowing the defence to a specific intent crime but not to one of basic intent. Rejecting the application of s.8 *Criminal Justice Act 1968*, suggests that evidence of intoxication turns basic intent crimes into strict liability. The reason given was that voluntary intoxication became an integral part of the crime, supplying the element of recklessness required in crimes of basic intent. This reasoning has also been the subject of much criticism (not least because of the problem of lack of contemporaneity).

---

**KEY PRINCIPLE:** *A defendant is reckless ("Caldwell-style") if s/he fails to consider an obvious and serious risk of which s/he would have been aware if not intoxicated.*

## R. v. Caldwell 1982

(see Chapter 2, p. 18).

**HELD:** (H.L.) Self-induced intoxication is relevant to a charge of intentional criminal damage but not where the charge includes recklessness. The fact that the defendant was unaware of the risk of endangering life due to intoxication was no

defence since the risk would have been obvious to him if sober.
[1982] A.C. 341

**COMMENTARY**
Lord Diplock held that the distinction between specific and
basic intent was irrelevant where recklessness was sufficient
*mens rea* for the crime. Whilst this decision takes precedence
over *Majewski*, it is restricted to cases where the defendant
has failed to think about the risk and its scope is now very
limited (see Chapter 2).

---

**KEY PRINCIPLE:** *If the effect of an intoxicant is not common
knowledge, the prosecution must prove that the defendant
knew the risk of its effect before Majewski or Caldwell can
be applied.*

## R. v. Hardie 1985

The defendant was convicted of arson being reckless as to
whether life would be endangered. He claimed to lack *mens
rea* due to the effect of valium which he had never used previously. He appealed against a direction that because the
valium was taken voluntarily it could not negate the *mens rea*
of the crime.

**HELD:** (C.A.) Appeal allowed. *Majewski* and *Caldwell* are based
on the premise that using alcohol or hallucinogenic drugs is
reckless because their effects are well known. There is a difference between drugs known to cause aggressive or unpredictable
behaviour and sedative or soporific drugs where such a presumption of recklessness is inappropriate. In the absence of
evidence that it was generally known that valium might render
one "aggressive or incapable of appreciating risks", the defendant could only be convicted if he himself appreciated this risk.
[1985] 1 W.L.R. 64

**COMMENTARY**
The principle from *Hardie* does not apply where the effect of
the intoxicant is common knowledge and the defendant simply does not know its strength: *R. v. Allen* (1988) (C.A.) (a
case involving home-made wine). Moreover, the outcome
depends on the charge and the anticipated effect of the intox-

icant. For example, the court opined that taking a soporific drug might be no defence to a charge of reckless driving.

---

**KEY PRINCIPLE:** *Majewski and Caldwell only apply to pleas of lack of mens rea. In deciding whether self-induced intoxication can be used in support of a defence, regard must be given to the law relating to that defence.*

## Jaggard v. Dickinson 1981

Whilst intoxicated, the defendant mistook a house for that of a friend. She broke a window to gain access and was charged with criminal damage. She pleaded a belief (*Criminal Damage Act 1971*, under s.5(2)) that she would have consent for the damage from the person whose house she thought it was. She was convicted on the basis that such a belief, caused by self-induced intoxication, was no defence.

**HELD:** (D.C.) Defendant's appeal allowed. The distinction between specific and basic intent was only relevant to pleas of lack of mens rea and not to the issue of defences. section 5(2) only required an honest belief and so even one induced by intoxication could be relied upon. [1981] 1 Q.B. 527

**COMMENTARY**
Whilst the court accepted that the crime (section 1(1)) was one of basic intent, the defendant admitted an intention to damage property belonging to another and the only question related to the s.5 defence. For this reason, the decision would not be affected by *Caldwell*.

---

## R. v. O'Grady 1987

The defendant was charged with murder and convicted of manslaughter after killing a friend following a drinking spree. He claimed that the killing occurred in self-defence. He appealed on the basis that his defence should be judged not only on any mistaken belief in the existence of the attack but also on any mistake about the severity of that attack.

**HELD:** (C.A.) Appeal dismissed. The defendant was not entitled, in any event, to rely on self-defence based on a mistake induced by voluntary intoxication. [1987] 1 Q.B. 995

## COMMENTARY

The court held that the distinction between specific intent (murder) and basic intent (manslaughter) was irrelevant because mistake was a separate issue from intent. Self-defence was no defence when induced by an intoxicated mistake. The same reasoning was followed in *R. v. O'Connor* (1991) (C.A.) (although the defendant's conviction for murder was reduced to manslaughter because his intoxication may have affected his *mens rea*). However, following *Williams* and *Beckford* (see Chapters 1, 2, 4 and 14), it is difficult to see why mistaken belief in self-defence is a separate issue from intent. According to these cases, such a plea is a denial of the mens rea of the crime charged which should mean that *Majewski* applies and the belief is relevant to a specific intent charge (*e.g.* murder) but not to a basic intent charge (*e.g.* manslaughter).

---

**KEY PRINCIPLE:** *Where a defendant deliberately becomes intoxicated in order to commit a crime, s/he cannot plead lack of mens rea at the time of the crime caused by that intoxication.*

## Attorney-General for Northern Ireland v. Gallagher 1963

The defendant was an aggressive psychopath, a mental disorder with latent effects which could be brought on by alcohol. He killed his wife having formed the intent to do so and having, possibly, consumed alcohol to get the courage for the crime. In his defence, he pleaded insanity and intoxication.

**HELD:** (H.L.) Prosecution appeal allowed and murder conviction restored. If a person forms *mens rea* whilst sane and sober and then gets intoxicated in order to commit the crime, s/he has no defence irrespective of whether the crime is one of specific or basic intent. [1963] A.C. 349

## COMMENTARY

The case also dealt with insanity. Whilst a disease of the mind (such as *delirium tremens*) brought on by intoxication might give rise to a plea of insanity, this was not such a case. Here there was a disease of the mind (psychopathy) which did not cause a defect of reason nor prevent the defendant from forming *mens rea*. The intoxication then brought out a defect of reason but because he had previously formed *mens rea*, he could not rely on this self-induced defect of reason to plead insanity.

# Involuntary Intoxication

**KEY PRINCIPLE:** *Lack of mens rea due to involuntary intoxication is a defence to crimes of both specific and basic intent.*

### R. v. Kingston 1994

The defendant committed acts of indecency which he claimed were due to him having been surreptitiously drugged. The judge directed that he could only be acquitted if the drugs caused lack of *mens rea* at the time of the crime. His appeal was allowed by the Court of Appeal and the DPP appealed.

**HELD:** (H.L.) Appeal allowed. The trial judge was correct. A defendant who had mens rea had no defence simply because involuntary intoxication caused him to lose control or to become less inhibited. However, where involuntary intoxication caused lack of *mens rea* it was a defence to any crime. [1994] 3 All E.R. 353

# Infancy

**KEY PRINCIPLE:** *A child between the ages of 10 and 14 is presumed doli incapax. This presumption can be rebutted by clear evidence that the child knew her/his action was wrong.*

### C. v. D.P.P. 1995

A 12-year old was charged with interfering with a motor vehicle contrary to *Criminal Attempts Act 1981*, s.9(1). He was convicted and the question on appeal was whether the presumption of *doli incapax* still existed and if so, what evidence was required to rebut the presumption.

**HELD:** (H.L.) The Divisional Court was wrong to rule that the presumption had ceased to be part of the law. To rebut the presumption it must be shown that the child knew that the act was wrong and not simply naughty or mischievous. [1995] 2 W.L.R. 383

**COMMENTARY**
The House accepted that the presumption might give rise to "anomalies or even absurdities" in modern conditions but that it was for Parliament and not the courts to change the law. The presumption only applies where the child is between 10 and 14. A child under the age of 10 is not criminally responsible and one over the age of 14 is treated as fully responsible.

# Insane and Non-insane Automatism

**KEY PRINCIPLE:** *A defendant is insane if suffering from a defect of reason, caused by a disease of the mind, so as not to know what s/he is doing or not to know that it is wrong.*

## M'Naghten's Case 1843
The defendant suffered from delusions. He was charged with murder, having shot and killed Robert Peel's private secretary.

**HELD:** (H.L.) To be insane, it must be proved that "at the time of the committing of the act the party accused was labouring under such a defect of reason, from disease of the mind, as not to know the nature and quality of the act he was doing, or, if he did know it, that he did not know he was doing what was wrong." [1843-60] All E.R.Rep. 229

**COMMENTARY**
This test is known as the M'Naghten rules. The case also establishes the presumption of sanity.

---

**KEY PRINCIPLE:** *A defect of reason requires deprivation of the power of reasoning and does not include retaining, but simply failing to use, powers of reasoning.*

## R. v. Clarke 1972
The defendant, charged with shoplifting, pleaded lack of *mens rea* caused by confusion and absent-mindedness resulting from, *inter alia*, depression. The recorder ruled that the defence was insanity, because of the mental illness from which the lack of *mens rea* arose.

**HELD:** (C.A.) Defendant's appeal allowed. Whilst depression might amount to a disease of the mind, the defendant was not suffering from a defect of reason because she "retained her ordinary powers of reason but . . . momentarily . . . acted as she did by failing to concentrate properly . . . " [1972] 1 All E.R. 219

---

**KEY PRINCIPLE:** *The defect of reason must cause the defendant to either not know the physical character of the act or to not know that it was contrary to the law.*

# R. v. Codere 1916

The defendant killed a fellow soldier and was convicted of murder. The defence raised insanity.

**HELD:** (C.A.) The expression "nature and quality of the act" related to the physical character of the act (not its moral character). Moreover, "not knowing that the act was 'wrong'" meant "wrong in law" or "regarded as wrong by reasonable people". Therefore, a defendant who knew what he was doing and knew that it was contrary to the law was not insane even though he might not understand that the act was morally wrong. (1916) 12 Cr.App.R. 21

### COMMENTARY

"Not knowing the nature and quality of an act" means that "he did not know what he was doing": *R. v. Sullivan* (1984) (see p. 145). Regarding knowledge that the act was wrong, a similar decision was reached in *R. v. Windle* (1952) where the defendant was not insane because he recognised that his act was contrary to the law (even though he may have thought that it was justified).

---

**KEY PRINCIPLE:** *A disease of the mind may be any curable or incurable physical or mental disease, of transitory or permanent effect.*

# R. v. Kemp 1957

A devoted husband struck his wife with a hammer during a temporary lapse of consciousness caused by the effect of arteriosclerosis (hardening of the arteries). Since it was accepted that he did not know what he was doing due to a defect of reason, the only question was whether the cause of the defect fell within the definition of disease of the mind.

**HELD:** (Assize Ct.) The defendant was insane because hardening of the arteries was a disease of the mind. The law does not distinguish between diseases of mental and physical origin. Either may amount to a disease of the mind if they bring about the relevant defect of reason. The condition of the brain is irrelevant as is the fact that the condition is curable or incurable, transitory or permanent. [1957] 1 Q.B. 399

### COMMENTARY
Any disease that affects the "mental faculties of reason, memory and understanding" falls within the M'Naghten rules. The definition given in the case received approval in *Sullivan* (see p. 145), subject to the important qualification imposed by *R. v. Quick & Paddison* (1973) (see p. 145).

---

**KEY PRINCIPLE:** *"Any mental disorder which has manifested itself in violence and is prone to recur"* may be a *disease of the mind.*

## Bratty v. Attorney-General for Northern Ireland 1963

The defendant was convicted of murder but claimed not to be conscious of his actions due to psychomotor epilepsy. He appealed on the basis that his defence of automatism should have been left to the jury.

**HELD:** (H.L.) Appeal dismissed for reasons given below. Lord Denning stated that not only were "major mental diseases . . . such as schizophrenia . . . clearly diseases of the mind" but so too were disorders falling within the definition given in the key principle above. [1963] A.C. 386

### COMMENTARY
This definition was doubted in *Quick* (see p. 145) and in *R. v. Burgess* (1991) (below) where it was said that a disease of the mind could exist even without a danger of recurrence. A disease of the mind can also exist without a violent manifestation.

---

**KEY PRINCIPLE:** *To amount to a disease of the mind, the cause of the malfunctioning of the mind must be something other than an external factor of transitory effect.*

# R. v. Quick & Paddison 1973

A diabetic nurse assaulted a patient during what might have been a hypoglycaemic lapse of consciousness caused by consuming alcohol and failing to eat after taking insulin. He pleaded guilty after the judge ruled that his defence, if any, amounted to insanity.

**HELD:** (C.A.) Defendant's appeal allowed. Any malfunction of his mind was not caused by "a bodily disorder" such as the diabetes. It was caused by external factors (using insulin, drinking and failing to eat regularly) and so did not amount to insanity. "A malfunctioning of the mind of transitory effect caused by the application to the body of some external factor . . . cannot fairly be said to be due to disease." [1973] 1 Q.B. 910

## COMMENTARY
The appropriate defence was automatism. The court felt that the width of the definitions of disease of the mind given in *Kemp* and *Bratty v. Attorney-General for Northern Ireland* (1963) (see p. 144) might lead to unacceptable results if not restricted to internal factors. The dichotomy between internal and external cause have produced surprising results. In *R. v. Sullivan* (1984) a man of "blameless reputation" involuntarily caused grievous bodily harm by automatic movements during an epileptic seizure. Adopting *Kemp*, the House of Lords ruled that the defence was insanity because it did not matter whether the impairment was organic or functional, permanent, transitory or intermittent. The position would differ if the impairment had been the result of some external physical factor. Likewise, whilst the defendant diabetic in *Quick* was held to be a non-insane automaton during the hypoglycaemic attack, a diabetic in *R. v. Hennessy* (1989) was held to be insane. In the former the condition was caused by external factors, whilst in the latter, hyperglycaemia was caused by failure to take insulin, stress and anxiety. Thus the Court of Appeal held that it had arisen, if at all, from internal factors (including the diabetes itself). Finally, in *R. v. Burgess* (1991), a man attacked a friend, possibly whilst sleepwalking.

Following *Sullivan*, the Court of Appeal held that this amounted to insanity because the cause was internal.

---

**KEY PRINCIPLE:** *Automatism requires proof of an involuntary act done whilst not conscious of one's actions.*

## Bratty v. Attorney-General for Northern Ireland 1963

(see p. 144).

**HELD:** (H.L.) Defendant's appeal dismissed for reasons given below. Lord Denning defined automatism as "an act done by the muscles without any control by the mind . . . or an act done by a person who is not conscious of what he is doing . . . an involuntary act . . ." [1963] A.C. 386

**COMMENTARY**
Unlike the defence of insanity which leads to a special verdict, a finding of non-insane automatism leads to an acquittal.

---

**KEY PRINCIPLE:** *Not every unconscious, involuntary act amounts to non-insane automatism.*

## Bratty v. Attorney-General for Northern Ireland 1963

(see p. 144).

**HELD:** (H.L.) Appeal dismissed. The judge was correct not to leave automatism to the jury. The only apparent cause of the defendant's involuntary act was the psychomotor epilepsy (a disease of the mind within the M'Naghten rules). Therefore the defence was insanity not automatism. [1963] A.C. 386

**COMMENTARY**
(1) Not only do insanity (internal cause see *Sullivan*) and automatism (external cause see *Quick*) differ in outcome, they also differ in burden of proof. As stated in *Bratty*, the burden of proving insanity is on the defence but the burden of disproving automatism is on the prosecution. The case also establishes that where the defence raise automatism, the prosecution (or judge) may introduce insanity.

(2) Involuntary act arising from intoxication is governed by the rules on intoxication and an act is not involuntary just because it is unintended or the result of irresistible impulse: *Bratty*. Examples of non-insane automatism given in the case were reflex actions, convulsions, lack of consciousness caused by a blow on the head, concussion, and sleepwalking. This last example is now incorrect following *Burgess* (see p. 145). A further example of automatism given in *Quick* and *Sullivan* was that of actions occurring whilst recovering from an anaesthetic. Moreover, in *R. v. T* (1990), the Crown Court held that automatism might be a defence when post traumatic stress disorder was induced by a rape (an external factor).

---

**KEY PRINCIPLE:** *Self-induced automatism may be a defence to a crime of specific intent but not to one of basic intent if the defendant was reckless in becoming an automaton.*

## R. v. Bailey 1983

The defendant was convicted of wounding with intent. He claimed to have been in a state of automatism caused by hypoglycaemia. He appealed against the direction that self-induced automatism was no defence.

**HELD:** (C.A.) Appeal dismissed. Despite the misdirection there was no miscarriage of justice. Applying the reasoning from *Majewski*, self-induced automatism could provide a defence to crimes of specific intent. Moreover, not every self-induced automaton would be reckless in the sense envisaged in *Majewski*. It is not common knowledge, even amongst diabetics, that the consequence of failing to eat after taking insulin can be "aggressive, unpredictable and uncontrollable conduct". Therefore, self-induced automatism (arising from factors other than drink or drugs) may be a defence to a basic intent crime unless the prosecution prove that the defendant was reckless in the sense of realising this likely effect of the action or inaction. [1983] 2 All E.R. 503

### COMMENTARY

In *Quick*, the Court of Appeal stated that self-induced or reasonably foreseeable incapacity would not excuse. The court in *Bailey* viewed this as *obiter*. In any event, *Quick* was decided before *Majewski* and *Bailey* brings the law on self-induced automatism into line with that now applicable to self-induced intoxication (see *Hardie*).

# 14. DEFENCES (2)

## Duress

**KEY PRINCIPLE:** *The defendant's will must be overborne by a threat of death or serious personal injury.*

### R. v. Valderrama-Vega 1985

The defendant pleaded duress to a charge of importing drugs. The defence was based on his severe financial hardship; threats of injury to himself and his family; and threats to expose his homosexuality. He was convicted on a direction that duress was only a defence if he acted "solely" because of the threats of death or serious injury.

**HELD:** (C.A.) Defendant's appeal dismissed. Threats of death or serious injury did not have to be the sole cause of the defendant's behaviour but only threats of that nature could amount to duress. In the context of the direction as a whole, the jury had not been misled. [1985] Crim.L.R 220

**COMMENTARY**
The threat need not be against the defendant. As this case illustrates, threats against one's family are also sufficient.

**KEY PRINCIPLE:** *The threat must be present and immediate, placing the defendant in an unavoidable dilemma.*

### R. v. Hudson & Taylor 1971

The defendants committed perjury, having been threatened with violence if they did not do so. They pleaded duress but were convicted on a direction that, the threat was not present and immediate at the time of the crime because it could only be carried out in the future.

**HELD:** (C.A.) Defendant's appeal allowed. Whilst the threat must be present and immediate, the injury threatened need not be capable of being carried out immediately. Moreover, whilst the defence may be lost by a failure to take the opportunity to render the threat ineffective, regard must be given to whether such an opportunity is reasonably open to the defendant, taking into account age, circumstances and any risks involved in trying to do so. [1971] 2 Q.B. 202

**COMMENTARY**
The court also indicated that one factor to consider was how effective (or ineffective) police protection might be. On the issue of immediacy, compare two analogous cases dealing with duress of circumstances: *R. v. Cole* (1994) (see p. 150) and *R. v. Pommell* (1995) (see p. 154).

---

**KEY PRINCIPLE:** *The defence cannot be used where defendants voluntarily place themselves in a situation which they know might give rise to duress.*

## R. v. Sharp 1987
The defendant voluntarily joined a gang of robbers, knowing of the leader's propensity for violence. When he tried to withdraw, the leader threatened to kill him. The defendant was convicted of manslaughter in the course of a robbery and appealed on the basis that duress should have been left to the jury.

**HELD:** (C.A.) Appeal dismissed. Duress is not available where the defendant voluntarily joins an organisation as an active member, knowing of its nature and knowing that pressure might be used to persuade him to maintain his involvement. [1987] 1 Q.B. 853

## R. v. Shepherd 1988
The defendant voluntarily joined a gang of thieves. When he tried to withdraw, he was threatened by a member of the gang who had several previous convictions including offences of violence. The defendant raised duress in defence to offences committed thereafter but was convicted after the judge withdrew the defence because of his voluntary association with the gang.

**HELD:** (C.A.) Defendant's appeal allowed. Where the risk of duress is freely undertaken there is no defence but the position differs where the group or member's propensity for violence was not known. The jury had not been given the opportunity to consider this point. (1988) 86 Cr.App.R 47

## COMMENTARY
See also *R. v. Ali* (1995) where the importance of knowledge of the violent nature of the enterprise or persons involved was stressed in denying the defence to a heroin addict who committed robbery to pay debts to his supplier whom he knew to have a reputation for violence.

---

**KEY PRINCIPLE:** *Duress is only available if the crime committed is one that the defendant was instructed, under threat, to commit.*

## R. v. Cole 1994
The defendant committed two robberies to repay debts to persons who had threatened him, his girlfriend and their child with violence if the debts were not repaid.

**HELD:** (C.A.) Defendant's appeal dismissed in respect of duress. The defence was limited to cases where the threatener "nominates" the crime and the money lenders had not stipulated that the defendant should commit robbery. [1994] Crim.L.R 582

## COMMENTARY
Whilst the threatener must nominate the crime, this may be done in general terms as in *Ali* (above) where the supplier had similarly threatened violence if debts were not repaid but had also handed the defendant a gun and told him to get the money from a building society or bank by the next day.

---

**KEY PRINCIPLE:** *The defendant must respond to the threat as would a sober person of reasonable firmness, sharing the defendant's relevant characteristics.*

## R. v. Graham 1982
The defendant was convicted of murdering his wife and pleaded duress based on a belief that his lover would kill him if he did not do so. He appealed against the direction that the test for establishing duress was objective.

**HELD:** (C.A.) Appeal dismissed. The defence is limited by an objective test which was "would a sober person of reasonable firmness, sharing the characteristics of the defendant . . . have so responded." [1982] 1 W.L.R. 294

**COMMENTARY**
This test is similar to that used in provocation (see Chapter 6) and was confirmed in *R. v. Howe* (1987) (see below). As in provocation, voluntary intoxication is not taken into account in applying the test. Nor are characteristics such as "unusual pliability or vulnerability to pressure" (*R. v. Horne* (1994)) or "emotional instability (and) neurotic states" (are not relevant *R. v. Hegarty* (1994)) since these conflict with the requirement of "reasonable firmness".

**KEY PRINCIPLE:** *Any mistaken belief in duress must be based on reasonable grounds.*

## R. v. Graham 1982

Above

**HELD:** (C.A.) The fear must be "well-grounded". In cases of mistaken belief the test was whether the defendant was "impelled to act . . . .as a result of what he reasonably believed had (been) said or done." [1982] 1 W.L.R. 294

**KEY PRINCIPLE:** *Duress is no defence to murder.*

## R. v. Howe 1987

The defendant and others were convicted of, *inter alia*, murder and appealed on three points. One raised the issue of the objective test in duress (referred to above), another raised the issue of liability of accomplices (Chapter 12) and another was whether duress was available as a defence to a principal offender to murder.

**HELD:** (H.L.) Appeal dismissed. Duress was no defence to murder as an accomplice or principal offender. *Lynch* (1975) was overruled and *Abbott* (1977) affirmed. [1987] A.C. 417

**COMMENTARY**
(1) According to *Lynch* duress was a defence for an accomplice to murder but, according to *Abbott* (P.C.), it was no

defence to the principal offender. In *Howe*, the House decided that no rational distinction could be drawn in terms of degrees of participation. Basing the decision on a number of grounds, including morality and policy, the House then followed *Abbott* and overruled *Lynch*. The court noted that their decision could lead to anomalies. Not least was the fact that duress might still be a defence to attempted murder and *Offences Against the Person Act 1861*, s.18 where the *mens rea* requirement was satisfied by the same level of blameworthiness as for murder and where the victim's survival could be by coincidence rather than design. Two of their Lordships suggested that the defence could also be excluded in cases of attempted murder. This was applied in the next case.

---

**KEY PRINCIPLE:** *Duress is no defence to attempted murder.*

## R. v. Gotts 1992

The defendant unsuccessfully raised duress as a defence to attempted murder.

**HELD:** (H.L.) Appeal dismissed. There was no justification in logic, morals or law for a distinguishing between a successful and would-be murderer. [1992] 2 A.C. 416

### COMMENTARY

Whilst the "sanctity of life" could not justify the exclusion of the defence from attempted as opposed to successful murder, the court was swayed by the fact that the mens rea of the offence required more "evil" intent than that for murder.

# Necessity (Duress of Circumstances)

**KEY PRINCIPLE:** *Duress of circumstances may be available as a defence where the defendant's action arises from a fear of death or serious injury.*

## R. v. Conway 1989

The defendant claimed that he drove recklessly because he thought that two men approaching his car intended to kill his passenger. He was convicted and appealed on the basis that necessity (acting in an emergency to save his passenger) was a defence.

**HELD:** (C.A.) Appeal allowed. Necessity could be a defence where it amounted to duress of circumstances (ie where circumstances constrained the defendant to act to avoid death or serious injury to himself or another). [1989] Q.B. 290

## COMMENTARY
The defence was not "pure" duress because the crime committed was not nominated by the threatener. However, the court accepted the argument from *Howe* that duress was a species of necessity. Whilst there might not be a general defence of necessity, in these circumstances the defence might be available subject to the same limitations as those imposed on the defence of duress.

---

**KEY PRINCIPLE:** *The circumstances must be such that a person of reasonable firmness, sharing the defendant's characteristics, would respond as the defendant did.*

## R. v. Martin 1989
The defendant drove his stepson to work whilst disqualified and pleaded necessity based on a threat from his wife (who had a history of suicidal behaviour) that she would kill herself if he did not do so. He appealed against the direction that necessity was no defence.

**HELD:** (C.A.) Appeal allowed. The defence was only available if "from an objective standpoint" the defendant acted "reasonably and proportionately" to avoid a threat of death or serious injury. The jury should therefore have decided whether or not the defendant had reasonably believed that he had good cause to fear that his wife would kill herself and if so that a sober person of reasonable firmness, sharing his characteristics, would have responded similarly. [1989] 1 All E.R. 652

## COMMENTARY
The test is the same as for duress. The court accepted that English law did, in extreme circumstances, recognise a defence of necessity in the form of duress and duress of circumstances. Moreover, whilst this and the previous case dealt with driving offences, it is clear that the defence extends to other types of offence (see, for example, *Pommell*, p. 154).

The case also establishes that any mistaken belief must, as with duress, be based on reasonable grounds.

---

**KEY PRINCIPLE:** *There must be a present and immediate peril to which the defendant responds.*

## R. v. Cole 1994

(see p. 150).

**HELD:** (C.A.) Defendant's appeal dismissed in relation to duress of circumstances. The facts did not establish an imminent peril. The link between the peril and offences was not direct and immediate as in *Conway* and *Martin*. [1994] Crim.L.R 582

### COMMENTARY

(1) The test seems more stringent than in *Hudson & Taylor* on duress. Also see *Blake v. D.P.P.* (1993) (Chapter 10, p. 108) where the vicar was denied the defence of duress of circumstances because writing on the pillar was not in response to fear of immediate danger to himself or those with him.

(2) The defendant must desist from the crime as soon as reasonably possible after the peril ceases to be present. Thus in *D.P.P. v. Bell* (1992) the defence succeeded where the defendant drove whilst intoxicated in order to escape from a threat of violence because he only drove a short way until a safe distance from his pursuers. Also in *R. v. Pommell* (1995), it was for the jury to decide whether the defendant, who took possession of a firearm to prevent another from using it, had acted as soon as reasonable in the circumstances when he failed to hand it to the police immediately.

---

**KEY PRINCIPLE:** *Necessity is no defence to murder.*

## R. v. Dudley & Stephens 1884

The defendants and victim were shipwrecked on a boat, 1000 miles from land. After nine days without food and seven without water, the defendants killed and ate the victim in order to save themselves. If they had not done so they would probably have died and that the victim, being the youngest and weakest, was likely to have died before them. The defendants were charged with murder.

**HELD:** (D.C.) Conviction affirmed. There was no authority that necessity (other than self-defence) justified a killing. Saving life by killing an innocent and unoffending victim did not fall within the scope of any defence known to the law. [1884] 14 Q.B.D. 273

**COMMENTARY**
The case suggests that it was not in fact necessary to kill the boy. However it appears to go further in holding that it would not, in any event, have been a defence. Despite suggesting that there is no general defence of necessity, more modern cases suggest that there may be (in limited circumstances). Nevertheless, it is certain that it would still be no defence to murder (see *Howe*, p. 151).

# Self Defence and Prevention of Crime

**KEY PRINCIPLE:** *A person is entitled to use reasonable force, at common law, in defence or themselves or another and also, under* Criminal Law Act 1967, *s.3 to prevent a crime or effect an arrest.*

**KEY PRINCIPLE:** *Whilst the circumstances giving rise to a plea under section 3 or at common law may differ, they also overlap and the legal requirements for both are similar.*

## R. v. Clegg 1995

A soldier shot and killed a car passenger and was convicted of murder following an unsuccessful plea of self-defence. The first three shots fired were, he claimed, in defence of himself or a fellow soldier. The fourth shot was fired after the perceived danger had passed and so, if anything, could only fall within the Northern Ireland equivalent of section 3 (force used to effect an arrest). In the circumstances the use of lethal force was excessive and unreasonable. One question on appeal was whether any distinction could be drawn between excessive force used in self-defence and that used in prevention of crime or to effect arrest.

**HELD:** (H.L.) Defendant's appeal dismissed for reasons given below. It was not practical to distinguish between the defences because of the potential overlap between them. The degree of permissible force and the consequence of using excessive force was the same in each defence, irrespective of whether the defendant is a civilian, a member of the security forces or a police officer. [1995] 2 W.L.R. 80

## COMMENTARY
It is not only the concept of reasonable force that is the same for both defences. The effect of the defences and the law relating to mistaken belief in the need to use force is also the same. Moreover, the burden of proof is on the prosecution in respect of the common law defence (*Palmer v. R.* (1971) (see p. 158)) and section 3 (*R. v. Kahn* (1995)). *Clegg* also illustrates that reasonable force can be used, at common law, to defend another (and oneself). It may also be used to defend property (*e.g. Scarlett* (see p. 159) and *Attorney-General's Reference* (1984) (see below)).

---

**KEY PRINCIPLE:** *For defensive force to be reasonable, it must be necessary to use the force in response to an attack or the fear of an imminent attack.*

## Attorney-General's Reference (No. 2 of 1983) 1984

The defendant was charged with, inter alia, having made an explosive substance (petrol bombs). He was acquitted on the basis of self-defence in that he intended to use the bombs to protect his premises from what he feared to be an imminent attack from rioters and looters.

**HELD:** (C.A.) The use of reasonable force was not limited to spontaneous reactions on being attacked. It also covered acts done in anticipation of imminent danger and could, therefore, provide a lawful excuse in such cases. [1984] 1 Q.B. 456

---

**KEY PRINCIPLE:** *It may still be necessary to use force even though the defendant has not retreated or demonstrated a willingness to disengage before resorting to force.*

## R. v. McInnes 1971

The defendant stabbed and killed the victim during a fight. He appealed against conviction for murder based on, *inter alia*, the direction that self-defence is only available if the defendant has done all he reasonably can to retreat before using force.

**HELD:** (C.A.) Appeal dismissed. Although the direction was too rigid, it had not misled the jury. A failure to retreat is not conclusive, it is simply one factor to take into account in deciding whether or not it was necessary to use force. [1971] 1 W.L.R. 1600

**COMMENTARY**
The court approved *R. v. Julien* (1969) which stated that there was no duty to retreat but that there was a duty to demonstrate an unwillingness to fight. This latter condition was held to be too stringent in the next case.

## R. v. Bird 1985

The defendant was convicted of wounding. Her evidence was that, at the time, she was being held by the victim against a wall and struck back at him in self-defence. She appealed against the direction that it was necessary that she demonstrated an unwillingness to fight before striking.

**HELD:** (C.A.) Appeal allowed. Failing to demonstrate willingness to disengage was, like failure to retreat, not conclusive but simply one factor to take into account along with the rest of the evidence. [1985] 2 All E.R. 513

**COMMENTARY**
The court agreed that failing to retreat or to offer to withdraw might establish retaliation, revenge or pure aggression rather than self-defence. However, this would not always be the case. Moreover, in "back against the wall" cases such as this, the fact that such evidence was not conclusive was of vital importance.

---

**KEY PRINCIPLE:** *If the defendant genuinely but mistakenly believed that it was necessary to use force, s/he is entitled to be judged on the facts as s/he believed them to be.*

## Beckford v. R 1988

An armed police officer was convicted of murder, having shot and killed the victim. He appealed against the direction that he could only rely on his mistaken belief that he was acting in self-defence if it was based on reasonable grounds.

**HELD:** (P.C.) Appeal allowed. Following *Williams (Gladstone)* a genuine belief that it was necessary to use force would negate the intent to act unlawfully. Therefore the test for self-defence is whether the force is reasonable in the circumstances as the defendant honestly believed them to be. The belief does not also have to be reasonable. [1988] A.C. 130

## COMMENTARY
This decision confirms the position discussed in Chapters 1 and 2 regarding the requirement of "unlawfulness" and the effect of such a mistake on mens rea. The same principle applies to s.3 *Criminal Law Act 1967*: *Morrow, Geach & Thomas v. D.P.P.* (1994). However, note the difference where the mistake is induced by self-induced intoxication (see Chapter 13).

---

**KEY PRINCIPLE:** *The degree of force used must be proportionate and no more than necessary in the circumstances.*

## Palmer v. R 1971
The defendant was convicted of murder, having shot and killed the victim, in what he claimed to be self-defence.

**HELD:** (P.C.) Defendant's appeal dismissed for reasons given below. The defence only applied where force was reasonably necessary. This depended on the circumstances of the case but a jury should bear in mind that "a person defending himself cannot weigh to a nicety the exact measure of his necessary defensive action." [1971] A.C. 814

## COMMENTARY
Consider also *McInnes* where the deliberate stabbing was unreasonable in the circumstances and *Clegg* where the use of lethal force against someone not believed to be involved in terrorist activities was "grossly disproportionate to the mischief to be averted". The court in *Palmer* commented that doing what one "honestly and instinctively" thought was necessary was, at most, strong evidence that the force used was reasonable. Despite apparent doubts caused by the later case of *Scarlett* (see p. 159), it is clear that the test for the degree of permissible force is objective.

---

**KEY PRINCIPLE:** *If the defendant makes a mistake about the circumstances in which force is used, s/he is entitled to be* *judged on the facts as s/he believed them to be in determining whether, objectively, the force used was reasonable.*

## R. v. Scarlett 1993

A pub landlord was convicted of constructive manslaughter based on an act of assault. He appealed on the ground that the act causing death was an exercise of reasonable force used to eject a trespasser from the pub.

**HELD:** (C.A.) Appeal allowed. Even an unreasonable mistaken belief that force used was lawful precluded the mens rea of assault: *Williams* and *Beckford*. Therefore the defendant could only be convicted if the degree of force used was excessive in the circumstances as he honestly believed them to be. [1993] 4 All E.R. 629

### COMMENTARY

The court decided that there was no distinction between mistakes relating to necessity (*Williams* and *Beckford*) and those relating to the degree of force needed (the instant case). The decision caused consternation because of a suggestion that the test for reasonable force was also subjective (*i.e.* that the defendant was entitled to use the degree of force that s/he believed was reasonable). However, it is clear that this is not correct. The force used must be objectively reasonable in the light of the facts as the defendant, subjectively, believed them to be: *R. v. Owino* (1995).

---

**KEY PRINCIPLE:** *A successful (or unsuccessful) plea under s.3 or at common law does not mitigate: it is either a complete defence or no defence at all.*

## R. v. Clegg 1995

(see p. 155). The first question raised by the appeal was whether a verdict of manslaughter, rather than murder, was available where self-defence failed because the force used was excessive.

**HELD:** (H.L.) If the defence succeeds it leads to an acquittal. If it fails it leads to a finding of guilty as charged. Therefore the defendant was guilty of murder because an unsuccessful plea did not mitigate the crime to manslaughter.

## COMMENTARY

The court expressed the same view that led to convictions for murder in *Palmer* and *McInnes*. Regret was expressed and various recommendations for reform were considered but, ultimately, the House held that any change must be by Parliament and not the courts.

# INDEX